HOW TO MASTER

In this Series

MASTER
GCSE ACCOUNTS

A complete practical course for students

Gwen Harlow

How To Books

Acknowledgements

The author and publishers would like to thank the examining boards named below, who have given permission to use exam questions from past papers. The examining boards are the copyright holders.

The Northern Ireland Schools Examination and Assessment Council very kindly provided the author with their marking schemes. The other boards are in no way responsible for the answers given. The London East Anglian Group accepts no responsibility whatsoever for the accuracy or method of working in the answers given.

In all cases, the answers given may not necessarily constitute the only possible solutions.

The London East Anglian Group
The Northern Examining Association
Northern Ireland Schools Examinations and Assessment Council

British Library Cataloguing-in-Publication data
A catalogue record for this book is available from the British Library.

First published in 1993 by How To Books, Plymbridge House,
Estover Road, Plymouth PL6 7PZ, United Kingdom.
Tel: Plymouth (0752) 735251/695745. Fax: (0752) 695699. Telex: 45635.

Typeset by Kestrel Data, Exeter.
Printed and bound in Great Britain by The Cromwell Press, Melksham, Wiltshire.

Preface

This book is designed to help students taking the GCSE Accounts exams. It will also be useful to anyone faced with keeping accounts for the first time. It is written with complete beginners in mind, and moves from the simple to the more complex in easy stages.

The text is kept to a minimum and is very direct. The best way to succeed in accounts is to have plenty of practice, so some exercises are included in the book with the answers at the back. These will be of great benefit and it is recommended that they are attempted without looking at the answers. The answers have been set out fully, as the layout is very important in GCSE exams. In fact, marks will be given for method. So if you only got one figure wrong in a series of figures you could still have almost full marks, even though your final total is wrong. You will gain marks for each correct part. It may seem at first that the book gives a very mechanical, simplistic view of accounts. However, as progress is made, the student will see that everything fits together. It is rather like the pieces of a jigsaw. The more progress is made, the more clear the overall view becomes.

There are different layouts for accounting procedures, and the most modern ones have been used wherever practical. Some of the chapters will not be needed by all students, depending on which syllabus they are taking. It is recommended that students obtain a syllabus from their tutor or their area board. A list of the boards' addresses is included.

You may have heard the terms 'book-keeping' and 'accounting' and wondered why there are two different names, or what each means. Book-keeping refers to the day-to-day recording of sales, purchases, returned goods and payments. Accounting is the bringing together of all these figures in totals. For example, the book-keeper will have worked out the total sales figure for a given period of time (probably one year) and the accountant will then use this figure to work out the profit. Various other total figures are also provided by the book-keeper.

In order to provide this information accurately and efficiently, it is obvious that there must be an organised system of book-keeping. The most widely used system throughout the western world is called **double entry book-keeping**. It is not a new idea. In fact, it was described in a text book written by an Italian called Luca Pacioli in 1494.

Double entry simply means that for everything recorded there are two entries. One will be a **debit** entry and the other will be a **credit** entry. Debit and credit in book-keeping do not necessarily mean the same things as in ordinary English. The debits and credits in the business bank account are the opposite way round from those found on the bank statement. It is a good plan, therefore, for the student to forget that she or he has ever heard of these terms. An open mind is needed.

This book begins with the **cash book**, which most students find easy to understand. It is then possible to relate back to the cash book when working out double entries.

If you have studied accounts before, you may wonder if certain items are being missed out. This is not so; they are all in there, but perhaps in a different order from that which you may expect. The book has been planned like a series of steps rather than one steep slope. Now begin a new and exciting journey into accounts.

Gwen Harlow

Contents

List of Illustrations

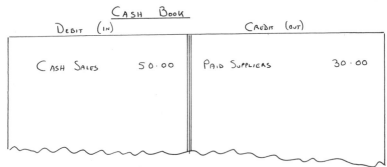

CASH BOOK

DEBIT (IN)		CREDIT (OUT)	
CASH SALES	50.00	PAID SUPPLIERS	30.00

Fig. 1. Cash book: debit and credit.

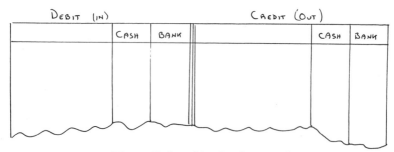

DEBIT (IN)			CREDIT (OUT)		
	CASH	BANK		CASH	BANK

Fig. 2. Cash and bank columns.

CASH BOOK

DEBIT (IN)			CREDIT (OUT)		
DETAILS	CASH	BANK	DETAILS	CASH	BANK
CASH SALES	50.00		PAID SUPPLIERS	30.00	
RECEIVED CHEQUE		45.00	PAID CHEQUE		40.00

Fig. 3. Debit and credit entries.

CASH BOOK

DATE	DETAILS	CASH	BANK	DATE	DETAILS	CASH	BANK
	BALANCES AT START	10.00	35.00				
APR 1	MRS. DAWSON		50.00	APR 2	MOWER REPAIR		30.00
APR 6	EMMA JONES	10.00		APR 10	PETROL	8.00	

Fig. 4. Writing up a cash book.

1
The Cash Book

The basis of accounting is money. Monetary transactions are recorded in the cash book. In some very small businesses, the cash book is virtually all the book-keeping that is done. The cash book is known as a book of **original entry**. This means that it is the first place where items are recorded. The cash book contains two accounts: the **cash account** and the **bank account**. Do not confuse this with the bank account held at the bank. This bank account is the business's own record. There are firms which use the cash book solely as a reference, and they keep separate cash and bank accounts elsewhere. In this book the cash book will be treated as being the only place where the two accounts are recorded. This is the most common method.

You will learn about other books of original entry and all the accounts as you progress. Do not worry if all these names seem strange to you just now. Students are often terrified at the thought of learning so many new things, but you *will* learn all that you need to know *gradually*.

WHAT DOES THE CASH BOOK DO?

The cash book records the money coming in and going out: the 'ins' on the left and the 'outs' on the right. 'In' is known as **debit**, 'out' is known as **credit**. If you have sold goods for cash of £50, you will enter the £50 in the debit (in) side of the cash book.

If you then pay your suppliers £30, this will be entered in the credit (out) side of the cash book. (See Figure 1.)

Some of the money will be in **cash**, some in **cheques** and other bank transactions. You will therefore have separate columns for cash and bank in the cash book. It will look like the example in Figure 2.

If you receive a cheque from someone it will go in the bank column on the left. If you pay a cheque out this goes in the bank column on the right. Suppose you receive £50 in cash sales, pay £30 to suppliers in cash, receive a cheque for £45 and pay a cheque to someone for £40. The cash book would look like the one in Figure 3.

Suppose Henry Smith runs a gardening service.

April 1   Henry received a cheque for £50 from Mrs Dawson for gardening work.
April 2   He paid £30 by cheque to have his mower repaired.
April 6   He received £10 cash from Emma Jones for work done.
April 10   He paid £8 in cash for petrol.
March 31   He had £10 cash and £35 in the bank.

His cash book for April can be seen in Figure 4.

Now try an exercise yourself
Enter the transactions below in the cash book for June. The opening balances (the amounts already in the accounts) were £30 debit bank and £25 debit cash.

June 1   Cash sales £30.
June 2   Paid rent £40 cheque.
June 5   Bought goods for cash £10.
June 9   Paid telephone bill of £50 by cheque.
June 11   Received cheque for £75.
June 17   Paid window cleaner cash £5.

When you have entered these items you have to **balance** them up. This means you add them up to see how much you have left. The way to do it is this:

● You rule a line across the bottom of the page, but leaving a line above it free.

● You add each column in the book, putting the totals in pencil at the bottom. The larger totals are the ones to be inked in.

● The totals must always be the same on the other side. If you have £10 cash on the left, but £7 cash on the right, you must ink in £10 total for both left and right cash columns.

● Therefore you will have some columns which add up to less than the total you have inked in.

This is what is meant by balancing.

You left a line free above the totals. Put in here the amount needed to make the column equal the total at the bottom. Look at the example in Figure 5; note that **c/d** means **carried down** and **b/d** means **brought down**.

The figure you put in (**balancing figure**) is always brought down to the *opposite* side. To do this, write the amount under the **totals box** on the opposite side, with the abbreviation b/d in front. The figures that are brought down represent what the business has in that account. In the example, the figures brought down are £12 cash and £50 bank, both on the left. Remember that left is the 'in' side of the book. This means that there is £12 in cash and £50 in the bank. Sometimes this figure differs from that on the bank statement from the bank. Your records will not always agree with those at the bank. There are various reasons for this, dealt with in Chapter 16 on **bank reconciliation**.

It sometimes happens that balances are brought down to the right-hand side, the 'out' side. If this is the bank column it means that you have overdrawn, taken more than you have in the account. This should not, of course, happen with the cash unless your cash box contains i.o.u. notes!

Fig. 5. How to balance a cash book

STAGE 1   CASH BOOK

DATE	DETAILS	CASH	BANK	DATE	DETAILS	CASH	BANK
	BALANCES AT START	10.00	35.00				
APR 1	MRS. DAWSON		50.00	APR 2	MOWER REPAIR		30.00
APR 6	EMMA JONES	10.00		APR 10	PETROL	8.00	
						?	?
		20.00	85.00			20.00	85.00

STAGE 2

DATE	DETAILS	CASH	BANK	DATE	DETAILS	CASH	BANK
	BALANCES AT START	10.00	35.00				
APR 1	MRS. DAWSON		50.00	APR 2	MOWER REPAIR		30.00
APR 6	EMMA JONES	10.00		APR 10	PETROL	8.00	
				(c/d)	BALANCES TO CARRY DOWN	12.00	50.00
		20.00	85.00			20.00	85.00

BALANCES BROUGHT DOWN (B/d)   12.00   50.00

An exercise to check your progress

June 1   Gemma Jackson has £30 in the bank and £5 in her cash box.

June 3   She received a cheque for £10.

June 5   She took £25 in cash sales.

June 6   She paid £35 cheque for her rent and had £10 in cash sales.

June 10   She paid a part-time assistant £20 cash.

June 12   She took £20 in cash sales, and paid her supplier a cheque for £40.

Write up the cash book and bring the balances down.

SUMMARY

● Debit = income

● Credit = expenses (outgoings).

● Totals of both sides must be the same.

● Balancing figure is brought down on opposite side.

DISCOUNTS

There is another main column which is included in most cash books.

Trade discount

This is a large discount given to other traders. It is given for two main reasons: bulk purchases, and to allow the other trader to make a profit. It is deducted from the customer's bill (**invoice**) before entering the invoice in the accounts.

Cash discount

Sometimes customers are offered cash discount for prompt payment. On the bottom of their bill (invoice) you may see the words 5 per cent discount if paid within 30 days. These terms vary of course, but that would be a typical one. It is *not* deducted until the customer pays. He will deduct it from his payment if he has paid within the time allowed. This is the discount that is entered in the cash book. It is entered in the **discounts allowed** column.

You also *receive* cash discount when you pay suppliers (if you pay promptly). This goes in the **discounts received** column.

- discounts allowed on the left

- discounts received on the right.

Think of their initials 'a' and 'r' and just remember that 'a' is first in the alphabet. You now have a three-column cash book.

So if Gemma receives a cheque from a customer for £19 in full settlement of their account of £20, they have taken discount of £1. If she pays a supplier £14.25 in full settlement of her account of £15, she has taken discount of £0.75. It will be shown as in Figure 6.

Note that discount columns are not balanced. The totals are entered in **discount accounts**. You will learn more of that later.

DATE	DETAILS	DISCOUNT	CASH	BANK	DATE	DETAILS	DISCOUNT	CASH	BANK
	CHEQUE	1·00		19.00		CHEQUE PAID OUT	0·75		14·25

Fig. 6. Entering discounts.

Exercise in using a three-column cash book
Enter the following into a three-column cash book.

June 30   Gemma's balances were debit cash £40 and credit bank £35.

July 1   She received a cheque for £38 in full settlement of a customer's account of £40.

July 4   She received £30 in cash sales which she immediately paid into the bank.

July 15   she paid a supplier £23.75 in full settlement of her account of £25.

July 20   There were further cash sales of £10.

July 25   She paid her cleaner £20 cash.

Enter up the cash book and bring the balances down.

There are further columns which may be added to the cash book to suit any individual firm's requirements. However, the three shown are the main ones. Once you are familiar with these, it will be a simple matter to add to them. Do not move on to the next chapter unless you have been successful in the exercises, and understand the summary above and the checklist below.

Contra entries

It is sometimes necessary to make transfers from cash into bank and vice versa. The entries you make in the cash book are accompanied by a small c. For example if you wish to transfer £50 from cash into bank then the entries you will make are debit bank and credit cash. Each £50 will be written as c50 in the cash book. It simply means that the entries are equal and cancel each other out. They are known as contra entries. See Fig. 8.

CHECKLIST AND TEST

1. What is the purpose of the cash book?

2. Are you able to enter and balance the cash book?

3. What do the balances tell you?

5. What is the difference between cash discount and trade discount?

6. How does this affect the cash book?

Check your progress

The following question is from the Northern Ireland Schools Summer 1989 GCSE exam. Note that the final part of the question has been omitted from here, but appears in the bank reconciliation chapter later in the book.

During the first week of March 1989 Mourne Enterprises had the following cash and bank transactions:

a. On 1 March cash in hand was £50, while the bank account was £1150 overdrawn.

b. On 2 March sales of £2,400 were paid straight into the bank.

c. On 3 March £28 was paid in cash to cleaners; also £1,000 owed to a supplier, P.Murphy, was paid by cheque.

d. On 4 March a debtor, W.Scott, paid by cheque £540, taking advantage of a £5 discount; on the same date £40 cash was taken out of the bank for office use.

e. On 5 March salaries were paid by cheque for £440.

Required

1. Enter the above transactions in the firm's cash book for the first week of March 1989.

2. Bring down the new balances.

3. Explain the meaning of the new balances.

4. Why is cash discount given to debtors?

5. Explain the meaning of a 'contra entry'.

(Answers to questions throughout the book are given in Chapter 21, beginning on page 128.)

2
Double Entry Book-Keeping

Double entry simply means that for every entry you make, there has to be a corresponding opposite entry somewhere else. This means that if you make a *debit* entry in the cash book, you must make a *credit* entry somewhere else.

Suppose that John Moss is going into business selling vegetables on a market stall. He decides to start the business off with £1000, and uses this to open a bank account for the business. The first entry will be debit cash book £1000. Following the double entry system you will then have to credit an account. The account you will credit is the **capital account**. The capital account represents what the business owes to the owner. This may sound strange, but is in accordance with an important accounting concept.

ACCOUNTING CONCEPTS

All accounting is done in accordance with certain principles or concepts. These will be explained as they arise in the course of the work. There is also a list in Chapter 22 for quick reference.

You have now encountered two concepts:

1. **Duality**. Double entry: debit and credit for every transaction.

2. **Business entity**. The business is a separate entity from the owner. This can be hard for many people to understand.

The business entity concept helps to explain why the business should owe John anything. Many people would regard the business as being John anyway, but this is not so. That is why John must always keep his own private bank account completely separate from that of the business.

So the first entries have been made. Now suppose that John decided to buy a second-hand van for £500, and pays by cheque.

The double entry for this will be:

- credit, cash book bank column
- debit, an account he will start and call motor van account.

The purchases account

Next John goes to a nearby large wholesale market to buy some produce. He spends £250, paying by cheque. The double entry for this is

- credit, bank (in cash book)
- debit, an account he will call **purchases**

The purchases account will be used to record all purchases *made for resale*.

Note that the purchase of the van did not go into purchases account. This is because the van is going to be kept by the business. It is known as an **asset**. Assets are such things as premises, motor vehicles, machinery, fixtures and fittings and furniture. You will learn more about these later. For the moment, just be aware that only *purchases for resale* (or materials to be made into goods for resale) are to be entered onto the purchases account.

Setting up different accounts

Now suppose that John goes to market and sells his produce for £320. The entry for that will be:

- debit, the cash book cash column
- credit, to an account he will call **sales**.

John now has to pay rent for his stall of £20. He pays cash. The entry for this will be:

- credit, cash column in the cash book
- debit, rent account.

He has now started a cash book and five different accounts. (See Figure 7.)

Note that the accounts can take one of two forms. In real life they are usually the **three-column, running balance** type. This has been so for many years now. Many people find the accounts easier to understand that way.

If you have to write up a lot of accounts just for an exercise, it

CASH BOOK (WITH CASH AND BANK ACCOUNTS)

DATE	DETAILS	CASH	BANK	DATE	DETAILS	CASH	BANK
	Capital		1000		VAN		500
	SALES	320			PRODUCE		250
					RENT	20	
					To c/d	300	250
		320	1000			320	1000
B/d		300	250				

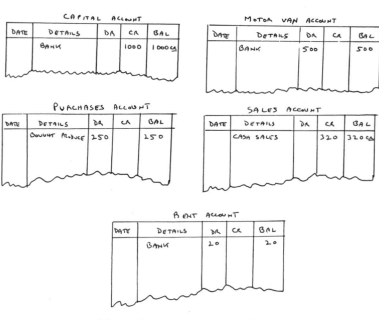

CAPITAL ACCOUNT

DATE	DETAILS	DA	CR	BAL
	BANK		1000	1000 cr

MOTOR VAN ACCOUNT

DATE	DETAILS	DR	CR	BAL
	BANK	500		500

PURCHASES ACCOUNT

DATE	DETAILS	DR	CR	BAL
	BOUGHT PRODUCE	250		250

SALES ACCOUNT

DATE	DETAILS	DR	CR	BAL
	CASH SALES		320	320 cr

RENT ACCOUNT

DATE	DETAILS	DR	CR	BAL
	BANK	20		20

Fig. 7. Cash and bank accounts.
Fig. 8. Making a contra entry.

DATE	DETAILS	CASH	BANK	DATE	DETAILS	CASH	BANK
	BALANCE B/d	300	250				
	CASH		c250		BANK	250	
					To c/d	50	500
		300	500			300	500
B/d		50	500				

20

may be simpler to write them with the debits and credits side by side, as in the cash book. You may do them whichever way you wish.

Contra entry
You will see that the business now has £300 in cash and £250 in the bank. John may decide to pay most of the cash in to the bank, say £250. The double entry for this will be:

- debit, the column bank
- credit, cash—out of cash into bank.

When making an entry like this in the cash book you mark the entries with a small 'c', as shown in Figure 8 and described in Chapter 1. The 'c' stands for contra. This is now known as a **contra entry**.

As you will see, the business now has £50 in cash and £500 in the bank.

Making the entries
Now see if you can make a few entries for John. Suppose he does the following:

- buys more produce for £350 by cheque;
- sells more for £515 cash;
- pays rent again of £20 cash;
- buys new scales and pays £150 cheque;
- pays petrol bill £50 cash.

How should these be entered? If you didn't get that right, go back to the beginning of the chapter and follow it through again.

CHECKLIST

1. Do you know what the duality accounting concept means?

2. Do you know what business entity means?

3. Only certain purchases are entered on the purchases account. Do you know what these are?

4. What is the double entry for cash sales?

DOUBLE ENTRY

PROCEDURE

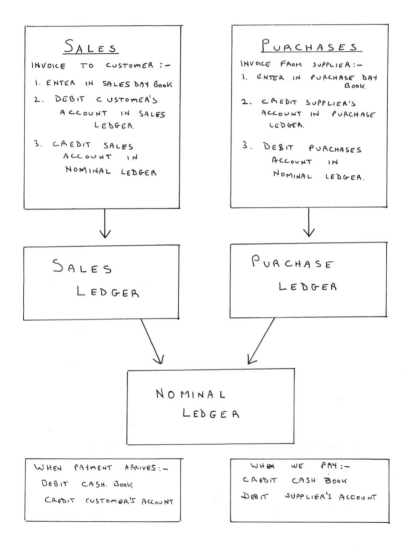

SALES	PURCHASES
INVOICE TO CUSTOMER :—	INVOICE FROM SUPPLIER :—
1. ENTER IN SALES DAY BOOK	1. ENTER IN PURCHASE DAY BOOK.
2. DEBIT CUSTOMER'S ACCOUNT IN SALES LEDGER.	2. CREDIT SUPPLIER'S ACCOUNT IN PURCHASE LEDGER.
3. CREDIT SALES ACCOUNT IN NOMINAL LEDGER	3. DEBIT PURCHASES ACCOUNT IN NOMINAL LEDGER.

SALES LEDGER — **PURCHASE LEDGER**

NOMINAL LEDGER

WHEN PAYMENT ARRIVES :—	WHEN WE PAY :—
DEBIT CASH. BOOK	CREDIT CASH BOOK
CREDIT CUSTOMER'S ACCOUNT	DEBIT SUPPLIER'S ACCOUNT

Fig. 9. Double entry procedure.

SALES AND PURCHASES ON CREDIT

So far all the entries made have been easy to work out, as they all went through the cash book. As you know which is in and out in the cash book, it was easy to know which side the other half of the double entry should be.

Unfortunately, life is not always so simple. People do not always pay straight away. This is the main reason for keeping so many accounts.

If you go into a shop to buy a jar of coffee, you pay the shop, take the coffee and that is that. The shop does not need to have an account for you. The double entry would be:

- debit, their cash book

- credit, their sales account (with the total sales for the day).

However, if you do not pay straight away for a suite of furniture or a television, the shop will need to keep a record of you. This will be an account in their **sales ledger**. The double entry would not affect the cash book. *You can only put items through the cash book where immediate payment is involved.* The double entry for the furniture would be:

- debit, the customer's account (in place of cash book)

- then credit, sales account as usual.

In your own accounts, your purchase of furniture would go into *your* purchase ledger. You would open an account in your purchase ledger for the shop you bought it from. The double entry in *your* accounts would be:

- credit, the supplier (in place of the cash book)

- debit, your furniture account. (Not purchases unless you were selling furniture in the course of your business.)

Study Figure 9 to see which ledger the accounts belong to. Customers in sales (**debtors**) ledger, suppliers in purchase (**bought** or **creditors**) ledger, and everything else in the **nominal** (or **general**) ledger. Some firms do split the nominal into assets (**real**) ledger and **expenses**. Also some firms keep a **private ledger** for the owner's capital and other accounts he doesn't want the junior accounts staff to know about. For the GCSE course, you will be relieved to know that you need only concern yourself with sales, purchases and the one nominal (general) ledger. The names in brackets are just alternative names which you need to be aware of.

An exercise in sales and purchases on credit
Sally Marshall starts a business as follows:

- began by putting £3,600 in the bank;
- bought some office furniture by cheque £650;
- bought machinery £550 on credit from Armitage Ltd (for use in the business);
- takings from cash sales £58;
- sold goods on credit to B.Wilson for £72;
- paid for the machinery £550;
- sold more goods on credit to B.Wilson £65;
- takings from cash sales were £350;
- bought another machine on credit from Armitage; Ltd £250, (also for use in the business).

The first entry is one you've done before:

- debit, bank (in cash book)
- credit, capital account.

Bought office furniture by cheque should also be familiar. The entry is:
- credit, bank
- debit, furniture account.

   Bought machinery on credit: here you must open an account for the supplier. You cannot put it through the cash book as you haven't paid yet. Instead of crediting the cash book you will credit the account for Armitage Ltd. The debit entry will be a machinery account. Note that you open a machinery account as the machinery is for use in the business. If it had been for resale you could have entered it on the purchases account.
   Cash sales entries are:

- debit, cash book (cash)
- credit, sales account.

Next Sally sold goods on credit to B.Wilson. Again you cannot put this through the cash book as he hasn't yet paid. You will have to open an account for B.Wilson. Debit the account for B.Wilson (instead of the cash book) and credit the sales account (just as you would for cash sales).

Paid for the machinery: the entries are:

- credit, cash book

- debit, Armitage Ltd.

The last three entries are really repeats so you should be able to work these out.

Fig. 10. Sales and purchases on credit.

DATE	DETAILS	CASH	BANK	DATE	DETAILS	CASH	BANK
	CAPITAL		3600		FURNITURE		650
	SALES	58			ARMITAGE		550
	SALES	350					
					To C/d	408	2400
		408	3600			408	3600

B/d   408   2400

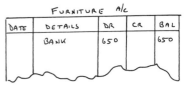

CAPITAL A/c

DATE	DETAILS	DR	CR	BAL
	BANK		3600	3600g

FURNITURE A/c

DATE	DETAILS	DR	CR	BAL
	BANK	650		650

ARMITAGE A/c

DATE	DETAILS	DR	CR	BAL
	INV.		550	550 @
	BANK	550		—
	INV		250	250 @

MACHINERY A/c

DATE	DETAILS	DR	CR	BAL
	ARMITAGE	550		550
	"	250		800

SALES A/c

DATE	DETAILS	DR	CR	BAL
	CASH		58	
	B.WILSON		72	
	B.WILSON		65	
	CASH		350	545 @

B. WILSON A/c

DATE	DETAILS	DR	CR	BAL
	INVOICE	72		72
	"	65		137

Exercises in double entry book-keeping

The best way to really learn double entry book-keeping is by lots of practical experience, so here are some more exercises to try. Keep your work carefully in a folder, as you will follow some of these accounts right through to working out their profit.

Mandy Baxter

Mandy Baxter decides to open a boutique. She:

- puts a £5500 cheque into a business bank account for the business;

- buys a second-hand till for £60 cheque;

- then decides to take £100 out of the bank for cash for the till.

- buys some dress rails and display dummies for the shop (which she is renting). She pays £1500 cheque;

- buys some new season's clothes on credit from Virgo Clothing Manufacturers for £2450;

- then pays her rent for the shop of £1200 by cheque;

- Her first week's trade is good and she takes £2350 in cash;

- she then decides to pay all but £100 of the cash into the bank;

- she pays Virgo Clothing Manufacturing the amount due to them.

Enter up all these accounts and balance off the cash book. Check your answer and, if correct (see page 133), go on to the next one. If not, go through the correct answer slowly. The notes with the answers will help you.

Harry Webster

Oct 1   Harry put £5000 into a business bank account.

Oct 2   He bought a printing machine costing £2650 paying by cheque.

Oct 2   He also bought some paper and card (to print for resale). This was on credit £100 from Alpha Products.

Oct 3   Sold some printed sheets on credit to Balfour Bell Ltd, £55.

Oct 4   He sold 20 printed leaflets to the Ladies' Luncheon Club for £23 cash.

Oct 6   He sold more leaflets this time on credit to Silverman Insurance Brokers for £72.

Oct 7   He bought more paper from Alpha Products on credit for £75.

Oct 8   He paid Alpha Products £100 by cheque.

Oct 8   He also sold some more printed tickets, cash £50.

Write up the accounts and see how much he has in cash and bank.

CHECKLIST

1. What items are entered on the purchases account?

2. What will the total of the sales account tell you?

3. Which ledger contains assets, expenses and capital?

You can now look more closely at one of the ledgers.

THE SALES LEDGER

The **sales (debtors) ledger** contains the accounts of the people who owe you money.

If you were to go into a department store, buy a sweater, pay for it and walk out, that would be the end of that transaction. To the store this would count as a cash sale. If you were to go into a local builders' merchants and buy 3000 bricks and a ton of sand, you would probably ask them to send you a bill later. The builders' merchants would then have to open an account for you. They would record on that account the amount that these bricks and sand cost. They would also record on it anythng else you may buy. This account would be in their sales ledger. This would probably be on a computer disc, but students find it easier to visualise the ledgers as sets of ledger cards. Each card is a **customer's account**. They are all kept in alphabetical order in a tray or box which supports them.

The entries for items the customer has bought, like the bricks and sand, are recorded as debits. A debit balance on a sales ledger account represents what the customer owes. The corresponding credit entry is on the sales account which is kept in the nominal ledger. That is how the book-keeper builds up the total sales figure.

When the customer pays any money towards this, it will be recorded in the cash book as a debit (remember the in and out sides) and the opposite (double) entry for this is credit the customer account. This, therefore, reduces the amount the customer owes. Note that the sales account is not affected by this. It remains as a record of total sales.

Any doubt as to whether an item is debit or credit can be solved by relating it back to the cash book.

The sales day book

There are two ways of entering invoices (bills showing what the customers owe) on to the ledger. In the course of an average day there could be hundreds of invoices to enter. The text book way to enter invoices is via the **sales day book**. All invoices are written into this book first of all. This is why it is known as a book of **original entry**.

You will see from the diagram of the sales day book in Figure

Fig. 11. Sales day book.

DATE	CUSTOMER	INVOICE No.	GOODS VALUE	VAT	TOTAL INVOICE VALUE
29 Sept	P. Jones	123	50·00	8·75	58·75
30 Sept	B. Smith	124	100·00	17·50	117·50
TOTALS			150·00	26·25	176·25

↓ To CREDIT SALES ACCOUNT

↓ To CREDIT VAT ACCOUNT

↓ INDIVIDUAL AMOUNTS ARE POSTED TO CUSTOMER ACCOUNTS AS DEBITS

11 that the totals for the actual amount and the **VAT** are totalled separately. The total amount at the end is what will be entered in each individual customer's account. The column showing the invoice total (minus VAT) will be totalled and this total will be entered on the credit of the sales account. Similarly the VAT column will be totalled and entered to the credit of the VAT account. In this way you can see that the debit (to customer's account) equals the two credits to the sales account and VAT account. The total of the other columns can be entered on to the **control account**.

Many firms use the following method. They first have someone pre- list the invoice totals. The accounts clerk may do this, or perhaps a junior. This means that the totals are added on a calculator which has a till roll, so that a written total is available and all the amounts are shown. Then the accounts clerk will enter all the invoices one by one, using a computer keyboard. When s/he has finished, the computer will give a total of all the invoices just entered. This should agree with the total on the pre-list. If it does, then that total is entered on to the **sales ledger control account**. Payments are similarly entered, but from the cash book, using the cash book totals as a guide. The control account gives the **total debtors figure**. If the totals of all the sales ledger accounts are added, they should agree with the total on the control account. Most computer packages will automatically enter the invoice total and the VAT total on to the sales account and VAT account respectively, and may also update the control account. The clerk does not have to consider this.

At the end of every month, a copy of their account will be sent to each customer. This is known as the **statement**, and its purpose is to encourage the customer to pay the amount owed.

When doing the exercises on double entry, you will have had more than one entry on your sales and purchases accounts. You can now see that the day book method would save time when entering by hand.

THE PURCHASE LEDGER

Note that the purchase (bought/creditors) ledger is entered in the same way, but with the entries the other way round. An invoice will be entered on an account in the purchase ledger as a credit. This is what is owed to the supplier. As far as you are concerned it is money going out. You can always relate to the cash book ins and outs. Remember that sales and purchase ledger accounts are

DATE	SUPPLIER	INVOICE No.	GOODS VALUE	V.A.T.	TOTAL INVOICE VALUE
1 OCT	J. WILLIAMS	632	42.00	7.35	49.35
2 OCT	B. BROCKLESBY	105	57.00	9.98	66.98
TOTALS			99.00	17.33	116.33

DEBIT PURCHASES ACCOUNT

DEBIT VAT ACCOUNT

INDIVIDUAL AMOUNTS ARE POSTED AS CREDITS TO SUPPLIERS' ACCOUNTS.

Fig. 12. Purchases day book.

just replacing the cash book entry until paid.

Just as you sent out statements to your customers, you will receive a copy of your account in their records from your suppliers. It is then the job of the purchase ledger clerk to ensure that this agrees with *your* records, before sending a payment to them. The purchase day book is almost identical to the sales day book. (See Figure 12.)

An exercise using the day book method
Mary Martin decides to open a printing business. She:

● begins by paying £6200 into a business bank account;

● then buys printing equipment from Touchwood Enterprises Ltd for £2300 cheque;

● buys some paper (for printing on to) on credit from The Paper Path Co, for £200 plus VAT;

● pays rent of £100 cheque;

● sells some printed leaflets to A.South on credit for £50 plus VAT on credit;

- pays the window cleaner £5 in cash;

- buys more paper from The Paper Path Co for £75 plus £13.13 VAT (on credit);

- withdraws money for her own use, £25 cash (called **drawings**);

- sells 200 posters to A.South on credit for £45 plus VAT;

Returns

When goods are returned, or you return them, do not enter them on the sales or purchases accounts. Instead, open special **returns accounts: sales returns (returns inwards)** and **purchases returns (returns outwards)**. Also use returns day books. Mary also:

- returns £25 (+ £4.38 VAT) worth of paper to The Paper Path Co, damaged;

- sells four packets of cards to M.Sugden for £50 plus VAT on credit; M.Sugden returns one of these packets. (Show these two transactions separately.)

- then sells 50 printed telephone pads for cash £62.60 plus £10.96 VAT.

An exam question

The following question is from the May 1989 GCSE exam of the London East Anglian Group.

J. Glendenning's purchases ledger contains the accounts of two creditors with the following balances:

	£
1988	
August 1 J Haryott	500
K Fellowes	670

During August the following transactions took place:

1988
August 4   Bought goods from J.Haryott on credit £1400.
August 5   Purchases from K.Fellowes on credit £890.
August 10   Returned damaged goods to J.Haryott £96.

August 14   Sent J. Haryott a cheque in settlement of her account at 1 August, less 10 per cent cash discount.

August 19   Received a credit note from K.Fellowes for £40 in respect of an overcharge on 5 August.

August 28   J. Haryott complained that the discount deducted on 14 August should have been 5 per cent and asked that the error be corrected.

Prepare the accounts of J.Haryott and K.Fellowes as they would appear in J. Glendenning's purchases ledger for the month of August 1988, bringing down each balance to 1 September 1988. (Answer page 138.)

SUMMARY

1. In debtors (sales) ledger, the invoices are posted as debits and payments as credits.

2. In creditors (purchase or bought) ledger, invoices are posted as credits and payments as debits.

3. Assets and expenses are debits (assets being things you own or are owed to you).

4. Income and liabilities are credits (liabilities being what you owe).

5. Purchases of assets are *not* entered on purchases account, but rather on an asset account (opened for the purpose if necessary).

3
Trial Balance

From time to time you will need to check the accuracy of your book-keeping. This must be done before preparation of the **final accounts** at the year end. However, it may be done at any time and many firms like it to be done every month, before the statements go out to the customers and payments are sent to the creditors. Alternatively it may be done half-yearly, or at the end of the tax year. It really depends on company policy and the time available.

HOW DO YOU DO A TRIAL BALANCE?

The way you check is to take out a **trial balance**. This is really very simple. It just means adding up all the credit accounts, then all the debit accounts and the totals should be the same. For example, you entered all the accounts for John Moss in the last chapter (Figures 7, 8 and 48). Now do his trial balance:

Trial balance for John Moss as at . . . (date)

	Dr	Cr
Cash	495	
Scales (Equipment)	150	
Capital		1000
Motor van	500	
Purchases	600	
Sales		835
Rent	40	
Petrol	50	
	1835	1835

You can see that his credits and debits both add up to £1835, so it seems that his accounts were entered correctly.

Now try to do Harry Webster's trial balance (see page 139).

If your trial balance totals do not agree, check the following:

- your arithmetic in totalling the balances;

- debits and credits are in correct columns;

- you have copied the amounts correctly—it's a very common error to transpose figures, eg 45 instead of 54;

- you have not missed any accounts;

- Arithmetic in ledger accounts is correct.

Author's tip

When balancing any accounts, if the amount you are out by is divisible by 9, then it is almost certain to be transposition of figures. For example, if the difference is 45 then you can work out that the figures involved are 27 written as 72, or vice versa (the difference between these two figures being 45).

USING SUSPENSE ACCOUNTS

Sometimes, in spite of all your efforts, you just cannot find the error(s) which are causing the trial balance to disagree. You cannot allow your accounts to disagree, but neither can you afford to spend any more time looking for the error(s). There is a solution to the problem. You open a **suspense account**. This is an account which you make up. It holds the difference in your trial balance totals. For example:

Trial balance

	Dr	Cr
Cash	25000	
Bank	20000	
Capital		40000
Debtors	10000	
Creditors		12000
Sales		47960
Purchases	45000	
	100000	99960
Suspense account		40
	100000	100000

The amount of the suspense account makes the trial balance agree. If you subsequently find an error, you must correct it using the suspense account as the other half of the entry. For instance, suppose that in the previous example the error was found to be a cheque received, and entered in the cash book, from B.Jackson for £440. It had been credited to B.Jackson's account as £400. To correct this error, you now have to debit the suspense account £40 and credit B.Jackson £40. This will put things right.

JOURNAL ENTRIES

You need to make a record of this, so that at a later date, perhaps when the books are being **audited** (checked by an independent accountant), it will be easy for anyone to see what you did. The place to record this is in the **journal**. The journal is just a record of events; it is not an account, nor part of the double entry system. The error you have just corrected would be shown in the journal with an explanation, as shown in Figure 13.

The explanation is called the **narrative**, and traditionally begins with the word 'being'. These days it is acceptable to just state the reason for the entry without the 'being'.

Fig. 13. Recording in the journal.

		DR	CR
6 NOV	SUSPENSE ACCOUNT	40	
	B . J ACKSON		40
	Being correction of cheque posted as wrong amount.		

ERRORS NOT SHOWN BY TRIAL BALANCE

By now you are beginning to realise that there always have to be snags with accounts. Unfortunately, the trial balance has its drawbacks. Various errors could occur in the accounts which would *not* show up in the trial balance.

Many students find this confusing at first. It must be stressed that the following list of types of error *would not be shown up by the trial balance*.

1. Commission (misposting)

Entered on the right side of the right type of account, but the wrong one. Eg, rent instead of rates, or perhaps B.Wilson instead of G.Wilson.

2. Principle

Entered on right side of wrong *type* of account. Eg, purchase of an asset entered on purchase account instead of asset account. (Remember John Moss's purchase of van.)

3. Omission

Item completely omitted from everywhere.

4. Compensating

An error has been made on both dr and cr which compensate, so that trial balance totals still agree. Eg, suppose an account has been debited with £150 instead of £200. Then another account has been credited with £350 which should be £400. You will be £50 short on the dr side, but also £50 short on the cr side so totals will still agree.

5. Reversal of entries

The entries have been made the wrong way round. Eg, cash sales entered as cr cash book, dr sales account (when of course it should be vice versa).

Original entry

The wrong figure used throughout, but all entries otherwise correct. Eg, a cheque received from a customer for £55 has been entered as dr cash book £50, cr customer account £50, (dr and cr correct—amount wrong).

Spotting errors in the trial balance

These errors must be learned and understood as the GCSE exams always contain some sort of question(s) on them. You are often asked to give examples, so you may like to think of some of your own too, checking to make sure they do not make the trial balance disagree.

Try the following. State what type of error is involved:

1. B.Snaith bought goods from M.G.Mason on credit for £36. This transaction was entered as a credit on the account of G.M.Mason.

2. A credit sale of £300 was entered in double entry accounts as £30.

3. A purchase of £250 was entirely omitted from the books.

4. When B.Smith paid the £50 he owed, you debited his account and credited the cash book.

5. When you paid £500 rent, this was entered onto the debit side of an account in the purchase ledger.

6. When a customer paid you £35, you debited the cash book but also debited his account with the £35. In the same period you debited an invoice from a supplier for £35 to the supplier's account in the purchase ledger.

If errors are discovered after preparation of final accounts, then it will be necessary to correct these also. Later in the book you will find worked examples involving the correction of errors, in conjunction with corrected **net profit** figures.

An exam question

Try this extract from an exam question, NEA 1989. (Ignore the part which mentions balance sheet.)

1. What is a trial balance?

2. What is the purpose of trial balance?

3. How does a trial balance differ from a balance sheet?

4. Name four types of error which will *not* be revealed by a trial balance.

5. Using *two* of your types of error as above, explain why they *will not* be revealed by a trial balance.

6. Write down *four* different examples of errors which could have been made in the books of account, and would result in the trial balance totals *not* being equal.

7. Explain the reasons why each of the following steps may be taken to try to trace the error when a trial balance does *not* balance:

a. Check any transaction with a value equal to the difference between the trial balance totals.

b. Check any transaction with a value equal to half the difference between the trial balance totals.

4
Trading and Profit and Loss Accounts

Working out profit is not as straightforward as you may think. Suppose you bought 372 books at £3.50 each, then sold 129 books at £4.75 each. How much profit will you have made?

Bought 372 at £3.50 each = £1302

Sold 129 at £4.75 each = £612.75

The simplest answer would be £689.25 (£1302 - £612.75), but this would be wrong. It is necessary to take into account the books (**stock**) you have left.

Another way to work it out would be:

129 x £1.25 (difference) = £161.25

That is the correct answer, but the way accountants work it out is:

● sales less **cost of sales**.

The formula for cost of sales is:

● opening stock (stock you have to start with)

● plus purchases (of stock)

● less closing stock (stock you have left).

To work out the stock figures you use the *cost* price of the stock. The only exception to this would be if the selling price was lower —obsolete/deteriorated stock sold off cheaply.

Sales		612.75
Less cost of sales		
No opening stock		
Purchases	1302.00	
Less closing stock	850.00	
(243 x 3.50)		
		451.50
Gross profit		161.25

This is called a **trading account** and is usually done at the year end. The title is very important. It is trading account for the year ended (giving the date) and also gives the name of the trader.

SUMMARY OF TRADING AND PROFIT AND LOSS ACCOUNTS

The title includes the words 'for the year ended'.

● opening stock will only occur if previous trading has taken place.

● Stock is valued at cost price (or selling price if this is lower).

● Total obtained is the **gross profit**.

● Stock is valued at the lower of cost or sale price because of another accounting concept. This is the **prudence (conservatism)** concept, which is that you must never overstate profit (or overvalue an asset). Always be cautious, even pessimistic.

A sample trading account

Now try doing John Moss's trading account, assuming he had £50 worth of saleable root vegetables left. You should have a gross profit of £285.

To take it further you must deduct **expenses**. It will then be known as a **trading and profit and loss account**. After deducting the expenses you will arrive at the **net profit**.

John had expenses of: rent £20 x 2, petrol £50. Note that the van and scales are not included here. They are assets. The expenses you want are just the day-to-day running expenses. So John's trading and profit and loss account will look like this:

Trading and profit and loss account for John Moss for the year ended—(date)

Sales		835.00
Less cost of sales:		
No opening stock		
Purchases	600.00	
Less closing stock	50.00	
		550.00
Gross profit		285.00
Less expenses:		
Rent	40.00	
Petrol	50.00	
		90.00
Net profit		195.00

MAKING ADJUSTMENTS

Sometimes certain **adjustments** have to be made to the figures used in the trading and profit and loss account. Occasionally people, or other firms, buy goods and return them for one reason or another. Goods returned to you are known as **returns inwards** or **sales returns**. If you return goods they are known as **returns outwards** or **purchase returns**. The sales returns must be deducted from the sales figure before working out the **gross profit**. The purchase returns must similarly be deducted from the purchases figure. For example, suppose a trader sold £50 worth of goods, then a customer returned an item worth £5. This same trader bought goods for £30, but sent back items to the value of £10. He had £7 worth of stock left. His trading account would look like this:

Sales		50.00
Less returns inward		5.00
		45.00
Purchases	30.00	
Less returns outward	10.00	
	20.00	
Less closing stock	7.00	
Cost of sales		13.00
Gross profit		32.00

There are other adjustments which may have to be made. When you buy goods, you often have to pay carriage and/or packing costs. These will have to be added to the purchases figure. Note, however, that carriage on sales is *never* shown in the trading account. All selling and distribution expenses are shown further down in the profit and loss section, under expenses. If there are warehousing costs, these are also added to the purchases figure.

SUMMARY OF ADJUSTMENTS

- Returns inwards (sales returns) are deducted from sales.

- Returns outwards (purchase returns) are deducted from purchases.

- Carriage inwards is added to purchases.

- Carriage outwards is shown under expenses in the profit and loss section.

- Always use labels: ie, cost of sales, gross profit and net profit.

If there was any **interest** received, or **dividends** from investments, etc, this would be *added on* after expenses. If there was any interest payable or similar charges, then this would be deducted. In that order.

SOME PRACTICE PIECES

Now practise some trading and profit and loss accounts. Some of them are questions from past exam papers and this is indicated. Don't forget the correct title—for the year ended, etc.

B.Burton's account
B.Burton's figures at the year end were:

Purchase	4850
Sales	10000
Stock at beginning of year	2950
Stock at end of year	3270
Electricity	500
Travelling expenses	420
Administration expenses	310

Write up his trading and profit and loss Account for the year.

N.Iveson's account
N.Iveson's trial balance was as follows:

Debit Credit

	Debit	Credit
Motor vehicle	1800	
Furniture and fittings	14000	
Capital		30000
Sales		15000
Purchases	21000	
Debtors and creditors	9500	8300
Stock	4500	
Expenses	500	
Bank	2000	
	53300	53300

Write up his trading and profit and loss account, using the figures you require. His closing stock was £3200.

N.Carter's account
After his first year of trading, Nathan Carter produced these figures:

Opening stock	10000
Closing stock	14000
Sales	25713
Purchases	19642
Returns inwards	235
Carriage inwards	242
Returns outwards	150
Salaries	4214
Capital	12000
Administration expenses	2231
Rent	3210

Write up his trading and profit and loss account.

An exam question

This question is from the London East Anglia Group exam paper May 1989.

The following information for J.Baker relates to the final quarter of 1988. Prepare the trading and profit and loss account for this period.

	£
Stock at start	5000
Stock at close	4500
Purchases	25000
Sales	37000
Returns inwards	250
Carriage inwards	750
Carriage outwards	1050
Wages (trading account)	9500
Selling expenses	750
Returns outwards	900

(15 marks)

Note that although wages are normally deducted in the profit and loss section, here you are told specifically to deduct them in trading account.

CORRECTED NET PROFIT

As stated in the last chapter, sometimes errors are discovered which were not shown up by the trial balance. This means that you will have prepared your trading and profit and loss account, so you will have to do a **corrected net profit calculation**.

Suppose Joe's Fish Shop's net profit was £1500. Then he found that his **closing stock figure** was £500 and not £445 as he had first thought. Also his purchases had been £155 more than the figure he had used.

The corrected net profit is calculated like this:

Net profit	1500
Add adjustment to closing stock	55
	1555
Less adjustment to purchases figure	155
Corrected net profit	1400

The closing stock adjustment is added because the closing stock figure used had been lower. Had it been the true value, there would have been more to deduct from opening stock + purchases. Therefore a lower figure would have been taken from sales to arrive at a greater profit.

Similarly, had his purchases figure been greater (as it should have been), then there would have been a greater figure to deduct from sales, making the profit figure lower.

To convince yourself of this, try a simple trading account like this:

Sales		6
Opening stock	5	
+ Purchases	3	
	8	
− Closing stock	4	
		4
		2

Now suppose his closing stock stock was 5 not 4. There would be 3 to take from the 6, so profit would be 3 not 2.

Now suppose that his purchases had been 4 not 3. You can work that through and see that it would reduce the profit.

Profit adjustments
Try the following:

a. If purchases were overvalued how would this affect gross profit?

b. If a gas bill of £434 has been paid, but entered in the books as £334, how would this affect the net profit?

c. If stock at the end of a period is undervalued, would this increase or decrease gross profit?

d. Suppose an item of £252 rent paid had been entered in the cash book, but the other half of the double entry not done, how would this affect the net profit?

An exam question

This is part of an exam question from the NEA Board 1989 exam. (The other part was used in the previous chapter.)

After the draft final accounts for the year ended 30 April 1989 had been prepared, the following errors were discovered:

1. Drawings of £400 had been entered in the profit and loss account on the debit side. (Answer: + £400.)

2. Stock at 30 April 1989 had been overvalued by £620.

3. The total of the purchases day book had been over-added by £680.

4. Returns outwards of £5000 had been deducted from the sales.

5. The provision for doubtful debts had not been increased from £900 to £1200. (Ignore for now).

6. No adjustment had been made for advertising prepaid of £400.

For *each* of these errors in turn show how the net profit would be affected *after* the error is corrected. In each cast indicate whether the net profit would increase (+) or decrease (-) and by how much. Number 1 has been completed as an example. (10 marks.)

PREPAYMENTS AND ACCRUALS

When you prepare the profit and loss account, you only want to include expenses pertaining to *that year*. This means that any **prepaid expenses**, ie paid in advance for next year, will have to be included in next year's accounts and not in this year's.

However, any **accrued expenses**, ie still owing at the end of the year, will have to be included in this year's account, as they have been incurred this year.

It often happens that amounts are split, because a firm's financial year may not agree with the times for paying bills. For instance, suppose you started a business and paid a year's rent in advance on 1 April. You have decided that your financial year is going to be the calendar year (you will do your final accounts to 31 December). This means that you will have paid three months (January—March) which you will not want to include in your accounts for the year ending 31 December. That will be a prepayment. You will have to *deduct* that amount from your figure for the profit and loss account.

Suppose you rent machinery and pay the rent quarterly, two weeks after the end of each quarter. On 31 December you will be owing the rent for that quarter (Oct-Dec). You will have to *include* that rental in your accounts as it applies to this year.

As the profit and loss is an account, the amounts are taken from the expense accounts to post to it. For instance, electricity: suppose you have worked out that the four quarters for this year amounted to £500 (perhaps this isn't what is on the account), then you will credit the electricity account with £500 and debit the profit and loss account £500. This way the adjustments are taken care of every year, and only that year's amount is posted to the profit and loss account.

SUMMARY OF PREPAYMENTS AND ACCRUALS

- It is the time when debts are incurred that is important—not when payment is made.

- The profit and loss account includes everything pertaining to that year, whether paid or not.

Try the following which includes prepayment and accrual.

N.Barlow's account
N.Barlow has a list of figures with which to work out his final accounts.

Sales	23000
Purchases	15000
Opening stock	7500
Closing stock	5500
Insurance	800
Electricity	650
Administration expenses	2300
Wages and salaries	16000

£200 of the insurance was paid in advance for next year, but £150 of the electricity had been owing (accrued) from last year.

Write up his trading and profit and loss account.

5
The Balance Sheet

The next stage is to prepare the **balance sheet**. This is really a list of **assets** and **liabilities**, showing how they were financed. Whereas the trading and profit and loss account is for the year ended, the balance sheet is the state of affairs *as at* a particular date. This is because the balance sheet is not an account like the profit and loss. It doesn't cover a period of time, it merely shows how things are *at that date*.

The correct title is: balance sheet for (name) as at (date). Begin by listing the assets.

WHAT ARE ASSETS?

There are different types of asset. The main ones are **fixed** and **current**.

Fixed assets

These are items owned by the business and which are regarded as fairly permanent; eg the premises, fixtures and fittings in the premises, motor vehicles, machinery, equipment and so on.

Current assets

These are the fluctuating assets: stock, debtors, bank and cash. They are listed in order of **liquidity** with least liquid first. Liquid, in the accounting sense, means transferrable into cash. Current assets´ are all liquid assets in that they are frequently being converted, directly or indirectly, into cash. They are constantly on the move. If you think of current as being the current of a fast-flowing river this may help you to remember what current assets are.

CURRENT LIABILITIES

The next thing to do is to list the **current liabilities**. Liabilities are items owed by you. Therefore the creditors figure is a liability. Strictly speaking, a current liability is a debt which falls due within one year, so a long-term loan is not a current liability. However, a bank overdraft can be called in by the bank at any time, and is therefore a current liability.

WORKING CAPITAL
The current liabilities are deducted from the *current* assets to give what is known as the **working capital**. This is a very important figure, and you will be sure to have to identify it for the GCSE exam. The working capital is then added to the fixed assets. The resulting total is the net assets.

LONG TERM LIABILITY
Any long term liabilities are labelled as such, and deducted from net assets total. The final total is then known as *net worth*.

FINANCED BY
You then have to say how the assets are financed, so list the capital, long-term loans, net profit and deduct any drawings. Drawings are money taken out of the business by the owner for his own use. The total should be the same as for net assets. Look at the example of John Moss's Balance sheet.

Balance sheet for John Moss as at (date)

Fixed assets			
Motor van			500
Scales			150
			650
Current assets			
Stock	50		
Cash	495		
		545	
Current liabilities		None	
Working capital			545
			1195
Financed by			
Capital at start	1000		
Add net profit	195		
			1195

SUMMARY AND PRACTICE

- The title must always include the words 'as at'.

- Always use the correct labels for totals, ie working capital, net assets.

Draw up a balance sheet

From the following figures, draw up the balance sheet of B.Bertram as at 31 December:

Premises	28000
Van	5000
Stock	4000
Bank	1000
Debtors	2500
Creditors	3000
Capital	30000
Net profit	8000
Drawings	500

Do not look at the answer until you have made a good attempt. This will be to your advantage—practice is the key to success with accounts.

If you've got that right, try the next one for revision of profit and loss accounts also.

G.Cooper's balances as at 31 December:

Premises	30000
Fittings	5000
Insurance	500 (an expense)
Van	6500
Sales	40000
Wages	5000
Debtors	7000
Purchases	30000
Closing stock	10000
Capital	59000
Creditors	4000
Rates	3000
Electricity	2000
Bank	10000
Drawings	4000

REVENUE AND CAPITAL EXPENDITURE

Now that you are doing balance sheets as well as profit and loss accounts, you may sometimes wonder in which of these a particular item goes. This is why there is a prompt in brackets beside insurance. So that you can work it out for yourself without any prompting, you will have to study the following explanation:

- **Revenue expenditure** goes in the profit and loss account;

- **Capital expenditure** goes in the balance sheet.

Revenue expenditure
Revenue expenses are those incurred in the day-to-day running of the business, such as salaries, electricity, insurance, purchase of goods for resale, maintenance, etc.

Capital expenditure
This is the purchase of fixed assets which will not be consumed during the accounting period (usually one year), eg purchase of new vehicles, fixtures and fittings, machinery, etc. These are permanent in accounting terms; will still be present next year. However, small inexpensive items such as staplers are counted as revenue expenses and shown in the profit and loss account.

It is very important to be able to distinguish between capital and revenue expenses as they have a direct effect on the profit figures. If you were to buy a new van, and charge it to profit and loss account, it could have a disastrous effect on this year's profit. The balance sheet would not show it as an asset, so that would be inaccurate too.

Sometimes the profit and loss account is called a **revenue statement**. Perhaps this will help you to remember where revenue expenses go.

EXERCISES IN BALANCE SHEETS

Try this balance sheet from the NEA 1989 Summer exam:

The following balances remained in the books of Jason Green, a sole trader, after the preparation of the trading and profit and loss accounts for the year ended 31 May 1989.

	£
Capital (1 June 1988)	89000
Drawings	6000
Expense creditors	580
Trade debtors	4000
Fixtures and fittings	12000
Expenses prepaid	800
Trade creditors	2000
Mortgage on premises	6000
Cash balance	200
Bank overdraft	1420
Net loss for the year ended 31 May 1989	1000
Premises	60000
Stock (31 May 1989)	15000

Set out the balance sheet of Jason Green as at 31 May, showing clearly the totals of the following:

● fixed assets

● current assets

● current liabilities

● long term liabilities

● working capital

● net assets.

(28 marks)

6
Accounting for Depreciation

One revenue expense not yet mentioned is **depreciation**. Assets wear out, or become less valuable with time. We all know that a new car is worth a lot less as soon as it has been bought, even when it has only been driven to the end of the street! It is no longer brand new. Each year it will be worth less. The same lessening of value happens with other assets, though not usually land or premises. However, a quarry or mine may be worth less as it begins to run short of its product.

It is sensible to account for this in the balance sheet, and profit and loss account, year by year. Otherwise you would have accounts showing that you own a lot in assets. This would go against the accounting principle of prudence (conservatism); the assets would be overstated. Accountants therefore spread the depreciation over the life of the asset. This depreciation is set against the profit in the profit and loss account as an expense.

It is rather like saying that your car costs you £20 a week overall, and not just the £5 worth of petrol you put in it. It may work out at an average of £5 a week to cover servicing/maintenance. The £20 includes £10 to cover the wear and tear (depreciation) as well. A brand new car would cost more in depreciation to begin with, but you may wish to spread this cost over its life. You could work this out using the **straight line method** of depreciation. This is one of three methods of calculating depreciation.

THE STRAIGHT LINE METHOD

The formula for straight line is:

$$\frac{\text{Cost less scrap value}}{\text{Useful life in years}}$$

Suppose you buy a car for £3500 and hope to get £500 for it in three years time:

$$\frac{3500-500}{3} = 1000$$

You would have to depreciate the car by £1000 per year. If you thought it may last six years, then you would have to depreciate by £500 a year which is close to the £10 per week mentioned above.

Alternatively, this may have been worked out for you and you may be given a percentage figure. If you are told to depreciate 10 per cent per year by the straight line method, this means that you depreciate 10 per cent of the original figure each year.

For example, a van costing £6000 to be depreciated at 10 per cent straight line:

- 1st year depreciation £600
- 2nd year depreciation £600, and so on.

It will be the same each year.

THE REVALUATION METHOD

A second method is simply to *revalue* everything every year. The depreciation is the difference between last year's value and this year's. For example:

- 1st year asset worth £8000
- 2nd year valued at £7500 so depreciation = £500
- 3rd year valued at £6100 so depreciation = £1400.

This is commonly used where lots of small tools, which are frequently replaced, are kept. An estimate of the value of them as a whole is used.

It sounds like a very exact method, but requires an expert valuation each year. The other two methods can be worked out by the accounts department without calling anyone else in.

THE REDUCING (DIMINISHING) BALANCE METHOD

A third method is to charge a percentage each year on the **reducing balance**.

This differs from the straight line percentage in that you are taking the percentage of a different figure each year.

For instance, the van costing £6000 is to be depreciated at 10 per cent using the reducing balance method:

- 1st year depreciation = £600
- 2nd year depreciation = (10 per cent of £6000-600) = £540
- 3rd year depreciation = (10 per cent of £5400-540) = £486, and so on.

USING THE DIFFERENT METHODS

Whichever of these methods is chosen, it must be the one used every year. This is in accordance with the *consistency* concept of accounting. You will see, after working out some examples, that each method gives a different result. If an accountant used a different method from one year to the next, a comparison of his final accounts would not be a fair comparison. It would be possible to change the method just before a proposed sell-out of the business, in order to make it look more profitable. When you have worked the following exercises, you may like to try to do them again using a different method. Of course you cannot use revaluation for this.

Try working with each method

Straight line
- Car cost £12000.
- eight years' life.
- sale value £400.

Reducing balance
- Calculate for first three years:
- van cost £10000
- depreciate at 15 per cent per year (round up to nearest pound).

Revaluation
- Cost of tools first year = £250
- valued second year at £215
- depreciation = ?

DEPRECIATION IN FINAL ACCOUNTS

Depreciation is treated as a revenue expense. It is therefore deducted from the profit in the profit and loss account along with all the other expenses. It also reduces the value of fixed assets and must be accounted for in the balance sheet too.

Balance Sheet for G. Cooper as at ... (Date)

	Cost	Accumulated Depreciation	Net
Fixed Assets			
Premises	30000 –	–	30000 –
Fittings	5000 –	500 –	4500 –
Van	6500 –	1300 –	5200 –
	41500	1800 –	39700 –
Current Assets			
Stock	10000 –		
Debtors	7000 –		
Bank	10000 –		
		27000 –	
Less Current Liabilities			
Creditors		4000 –	
			23000 –
			62700 –
Financed By:			
Capital at Start	59000 –		
Add Net Profit	7700 –		
		66700 –	
Less Drawings		4000 –	
			62700 –

Fig. 14. Balance sheet showing depreciation.

An example to look at

Look at the accounts of G.Cooper which you did in the chapter on balance sheets (page 145). Suppose that the fittings were depreciated by 10 per cent straight line, and the van by 20 per cent straight line. The expenses in the profit and loss account will now include £500 depreciation on fittings and £1300 depreciation on van.

Profit and loss account for G.Cooper for the year ended (date)

Sales		40000
Purchases	30000	
-Closing stock	10000	
	———	
Cost of sales		20000
		———
Gross profit		20000
Insurance	500	
Wages	5000	
Rates	3000	
Electricity	2000	
Depreciation:		
Van	1300	
Fittings	500	
	———	
		12300
		———
Net profit		7700

The balance sheet would have a special column for depreciation, as shown in Figure 14.

In the second year the depreciation will include both years' depreciation. (This only applies to the balance sheet—remember that the profit and loss account contains only items pertaining to that year.)

Balance sheet extract from the following year:

	Cost	Accumulated depreciation	Net
Fixed assets			
Premises	30000	—	30000
Fittings	5000	1000	4000
Van	6500	2600	3900
	———	———	———
	41500	3600	37900
	———	———	———

Note that the cost and depreciation columns are ruled off and not added in.

SUMMARY OF THE DIFFERENT METHODS

- With the straight line method the depreciation is the same each year.

- Only that year's depreciation is entered in the profit and loss account.

- The accumulated depreciation is shown in the balance sheet.

BOOK-KEEPING FOR DEPRECIATION

There are two ways of entering depreciation in your book-keeping system.

One way is to just keep entering the depreciation on the asset account. For instance, in the example above G.Cooper could enter the depreciation on his van account, as shown in Figure 15.

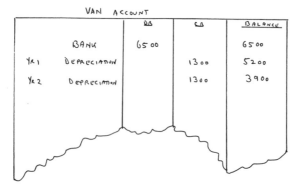

Fig. 15. Entering depreciation on the asset account.

Provision for depreciation account

Another way to do it is to have a separate account for depreciation. This way the van account can still show the cost of the van. This extra account will be called the **provision for depreciation account**. It will show the accumulated depreciation on the van.

The word provision is misleading. It would be better if the account was called the accumulated depreciation account. It in no way provides anything. It is not to replace assets, it is merely to avoid overstating the value of assets.

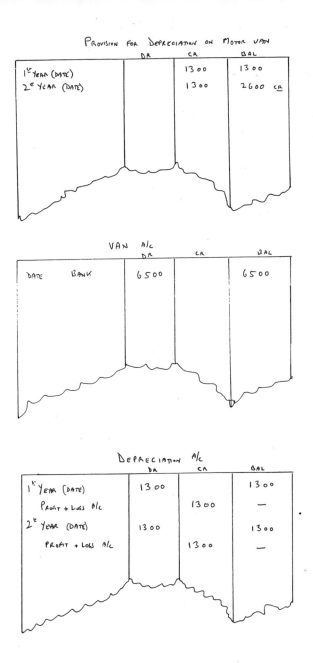

PROVISION FOR DEPRECIATION ON MOTOR VAN

	DR	CR	BAL
1st Year (DATE)		1300	1300
2nd Year (DATE)		1300	2600 CR

VAN A/c

		DR	CR	BAL
DATE	BANK	6500		6500

DEPRECIATION A/c

	DR	CR	BAL
1st Year (DATE)	1300		1300
Profit + Loss A/c		1300	—
2nd Year (DATE)	1300		1300
Profit + Loss A/c		1300	—

Fig. 16. Provision for depreciation on a motor van. There would also be depreciation on fittings or any other depreciating assets on this last account.

Depreciation account

In addition to this, you have to open a **depreciation account**. This will show just the year's depreciation, which will be transferred to the profit and loss account each year. The account will therefore never have more than that year's depreciation on it. (See Figure 16.)

This may sound confusing, but just remember that the provision account is the one with the amount for the balance sheet. The depreciation account is the one with the balance for profit and loss account.

Now try these

Z. and G. Castings' account

Write up the provision for depreciation account for Z. and G.Castings for the first three years:

- they bought a machine for £3000.
- They depreciated it by 20 per cent per year on the reducing balance.

Also show how the entries would appear in the balance sheet for the three years (short extract only).

AB Engineering

- they bought a machine for £20000.
- depreciate at 10 per cent straight line for the first three years.

Show the balance sheet extract for each year. How much will appear in the profit and loss account each year?

DISPOSAL ACCOUNTS

There is a special way of accounting for the sale of assets. It is simply to open a **disposal account**, and transfer everything pertaining to the asset on to it.

Suppose AB Engineering were to sell their machine at the end of the three years for £10500. They would first credit the machine account and then open a disposal account, debiting the amount to it. Then they would debit the provision for depreciation account, and credit this amount to the disposal account. Then when they got the money for the machine, they would debit the cash book and credit the disposal account.

Whatever amount is left on the disposal account will be transferred to the profit and loss account that year. (See Figure 17.)

If AB Engineering had sold the machine for £15000, however, the amount to transfer to the profit and loss account would be a credit. They would have made a profit on the sale, so the amount would be credited (added to) the profit and loss account rather than debited (deducted like expenses).

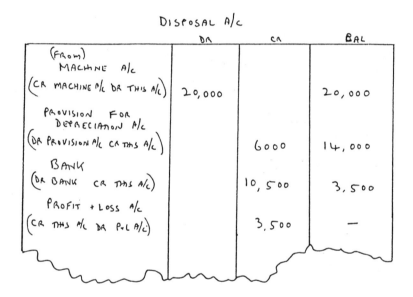

Fig. 17. A disposal account.

7
Bad Debts

The sales ledger is always bound to show accounts which will never be paid. Some customers will have gone bankrupt, perhaps some dispute their account and so on. Some of these debts are not worth spending money to recover. You don't want to show in your final accounts, year after year, that you have a current asset (debtors) of a certain sum if this is not recoverable. This would not be in line with the prudence (conservatism) concept of accounting. Of course this means that the book-keeping is going to be even more complicated.

If you decide to write off a debt altogether you must deduct it from the profit in the profit and loss account. Supposing you are quite certain that G. Glover will never pay you the £50 he owes, you have to write it off in two steps.

BAD DEBTS ACCOUNT

The first thing to do is to open a **bad debts account**. Then transfer the debt to it, by crediting G. Glover account £50 and debiting the bad debt account £50. This has cleared Glover's account and transferred the debt to the bad debt account.

At the end of the year you have to transfer the debt to the profit and loss account. By this time, there may have been other amounts entered on the bad debts account. The bad debts account is credited for the amount on it, and this same amount is debited to the profit and loss account.

Suppose that the £50 was the only amount that year. The bad debts account would be credited with £50 and the profit and loss account would be debited with the £50.

The bad debts account holds the debts until they are written off to the profit and loss account. Therefore this account will reduce to nil each year end.

PROVISION FOR BAD DEBTS

A prudent accountant should provide for the possibility of bad
debts, rather than wait for them to have to be written off. This is
because he will otherwise be overstating the profits and the worth
of the business. If say 7 per cent of debts are doubtful, then you
will be overstating the worth of the business by that 7 per cent.
To provide for the doubtful debts, open a **provision for bad
(doubtful) debts account**.

You have to decide what percentage of your debtors will not
pay. Suppose you have a total debtors figure of £5000, and decide
to provide for 5 per cent bad debts. The provision account will
show a credit of £250. The double entry is:

- credit, provision for bad debts account
- debit, profit and loss account.

Suppose in year two your total debtors figure is £6000. You will
need to have a provision of £300. The provision account already
shows £250, so only £50 needs to be *debited* to the profit and loss
account, as in Figure 18.

Suppose that in the third year the debtors figure is only £4000:
the provision needed is £200. That year £100 will be *credited* to
the profit and loss account, as in Figure 19.

Treatment in the balance sheet

Each year, the provision must be deducted from the debtors figure
in the balance sheet. Using the above example, in year one £250
would have been deducted, in year two £300 and in year three
£200. (See Figure 20.)

SUMMARY AND PRACTICE

- Bad debts account is only for accounts actually written off.
- Percentage decided must be same each year—consistency concept.
- Provision for bad debts appears in the balance sheet as a direct
  percentage of that year's debtors.
- The provision appears in the profit and loss account as the
  amount needed to bring the provision account to its correct
  total.
- The balance on the provision account should be the percentage
  required of that year's debtors.

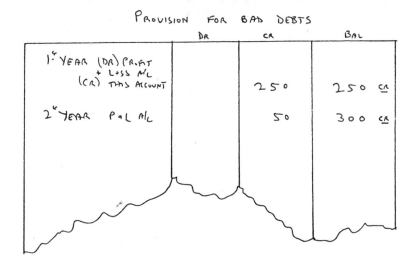

Fig. 18. Debiting provision for bad debts.

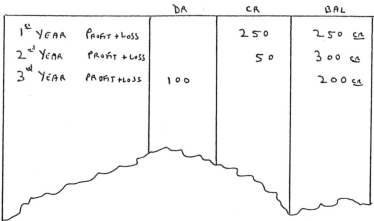

Fig. 19. Crediting provision for bad debts.

Now try some exercises

B.Taggart's debtors

B.Taggart has a total debtors figure of £5750. He finds that he will have to write off £750. He would like to provide 7 per cent for bad debts on the remainder of his debtors.

Write up the bad debts account and provision for bad debts account. Show balance sheet extracts, and the amounts which will be entered in the profit and loss accounts.

M.Bedwin's debtors
M.Bedwin had debtors of £3630 in 1988, £4720 in 1989 and £5940 in 1990. Write up the provision for bad debts (5 per cent per year). Also show the amounts which would appear in the profit and loss account and do balance sheet extracts for the three years.

M.Cox's debtors
M.Cox had debtors of £3226 in 1988, £5240 in 1989 and £5620 in 1990. In 1989 he wrote off £326 in bad debts. After doing this he decided to provide for 10 per cent bad debts from 1989 onwards.
  Write up all his accounts as for the previous question.

Fig. 20. Bad debts provision in the balance sheet.

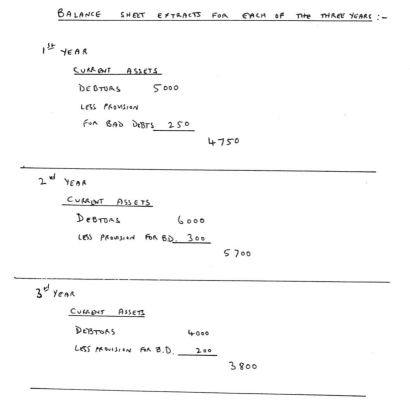

BALANCE SHEET EXTRACTS FOR EACH OF THE THREE YEARS :-

1ST YEAR

  CURRENT ASSETS
    DEBTORS   5000
    LESS PROVISION
    FOR BAD DEBTS   250
                          4750

2ND YEAR

  CURRENT ASSETS
    DEBTORS   6000
    LESS PROVISION FOR B.D. 300
                          5700

3RD YEAR

  CURRENT ASSETS
    DEBTORS   4000
    LESS PROVISION FOR B.D.   200
                          3800

8
Manufacturing Accounts

Many businesses don't just buy things and then sell them again. They buy in raw materials, make these into something else, then sell them. These businesses have to prepare an extra account, before the profit and loss account. It is called a **manufacturing account**.

PRIME COST

The first part of the account deals with **prime costs**. These are any costs which are directly involved in the manufacture of the goods, eg raw materials, wages of assembly workers.

Another direct cost is **royalties**. This is the amount paid to the patent holder for each item produced. As it relates exactly to each item, it is directly attributable to manufacture and so is a direct cost.

PRODUCTION COST

The other, indirect, costs are called **production costs**. These include things like repairs to machinery and wages of the factory nurse. Although necessary for production they are not directly concerned with the finished product.

WORKING OUT THE TYPES OF COST

Study the following list and see if you can decide which are prime and which are production costs:

- haulage costs bringing raw materials;
- wages of machine operators in factory;
- cost of raw materials;
- repairs to machinery;
- wages of maintenance staff in factory;

- salary of factory nurse;
- wages of assembly workers;
- insurance for factory;
- oil for factory machines;
- depreciation of factory machinery.

An example
The following figures are for G. Gladwin Ltd:

Stock of raw materials in January	500
Stock of raw materials in December (same year)	700
Purchases of raw materials	8000
Direct wages	21000
Factory rent (not including offices)	440
Royalties	150
Depreciation on factory machinery	400
Indirect wages	9000
General factory expenses (indirect)	310

The account will be laid out like this:

Manufacturing account for G. Gladwin for the year ended (date)

Stock of raw materials in January	500	
+ Purchases	8000	
	————	
		8500
Less stock of raw materials, December		700
		————
Cost of raw materials consumed		7800
Direct wages	21000	
Royalties	150	
	————	
		21150
		————
Prime cost		28950
Factory overheads		
Rent	440	
Indirect wages	9000	
Indirect expenses	310	
Depreciation	400	
	————	
		10150
		————
Production cost of completed goods		39100

Note the labels of the totals throughout the account: **cost of raw materials consumed, prime cost** and **production cost of finished goods**. It is very important to use these labels. In an exam question you may well be asked to show them, in which case it would be a good idea to underline your wording for them. You will notice they are in italics in the example of G.Gladwin.

SUMMARY AND PRACTICE

● Prime costs are the direct costs.

● Production costs are the indirect costs.

● Always use labels of totals.

A manufacturing account
Now try the following manufacturing account:

Stock of raw materials at start	650
Stock of raw materials at end	700
Purchases of raw materials	1000
Factory rent	900
Depreciation of machinery	400
Direct wages	3000
Maintenance wages	2000
Royalties	300
Parts for machine repairs	100

WORK IN PROGRESS

In the factory, at any given time, there will not just be finished goods at one end and the raw materials at the other. There are bound to be half-finished goods somewhere along the line. These are called **work in progress**. When working out the production cost, you have to take them into account. They are obviously worth something. The way to account for them is very simple; you just add **work in progress at start** and take off **work in progress at end**. This will give the value of work in progress during the period. You don't have to worry about working out the value of the work in progress at start and end. This will have been done for you.

Suppose G.Gladwin had £13200 work in progress at start and £13000 at end. This would appear like this in his account:

	39100
Add work in progress at start	13200
	52300
Less work in progress at end	13000
Production cost of completed goods	39300

The next thing you need to know is how to progress from this account to the trading and profit and loss account. A lot of students seem to forget this part so it's a good idea to pay particular attention to it.

Suppose Gladwin has the following figures in addition to the above:

Sales	62000
Opening stock of finished goods	17500
Closing stock of finished goods	13750
Salaries of office staff	5000
Commission of salesmen	6500
Tax and insurance for delivery van	400

His trading and profit and loss account would be as shown in Figure 21.

Fig. 21. From manufacturing to profit and loss account.

Profit and Loss Account for G. Gladwin for the year ended... (date)

Sales			62000
Opening stock finished goods	17500		
Add Production cost finished goods	39300		

		56800	
Less closing stock finished goods		13750	

Cost of sales			43050

Gross profit			18950
Less expenses			
Salaries of office staff	5000		
Commission for salesmen	6500		
Tax & Ins. for van	400		

			11900

Net profit			7050

Now you try one

B.Best's account
Do the manufacturing and trading and profit and loss account from
the following figures for B.Best:

Stock of raw materials at start	3000
Purchases of raw materials	9000
Stock of raw materials at end	4000
Carriage costs of bringing raw materials	500
Direct wages	7000
Indirect factory expenses	3000
Canteen expenses (factory)	1000
Sales	40000
Opening stock of finished goods	5000
Closing stock of finished goods	3500
Administration expenses	6000
Selling and distribution expenses	7500
Depreciation of office equipment	500
Provision for bad debts	350

9
How to Do Club Accounts

The title really should be 'The Accounts of Non-Profit Making Organisations'. Rather a mouthful, but it describes the main difference between these accounts and business accounts. The purpose of a club is the enjoyment and benefit of its members, not to make a profit.

RECEIPTS AND PAYMENTS ACCOUNT

Most club treasurers will keep lists of **receipts** and **payments**. This may be just the cash book. It will only record the *actual* amounts received and paid. You know, from your knowledge of profit and loss accounts, that when accounting for a period you must include any amount *relating* to that period. This is regardless of whether it is paid or not. Therefore the receipts and payments account is not sufficient in itself. You have to prepare another account.

INCOME AND EXPENDITURE ACCOUNT

The trading and profit and loss account would be inappropriate, so you prepare an **income and expenditure account** instead. This is really just two lists:

● firstly the income
● then the expenditure.

The result is called either the **surplus** or **deficit**. If income is greater it's a surplus, if not, a deficit. If there are items on both lists which relate to each other, it is good practice to put them together in whichever list they will then apply to. For example, if there are receipts from dance tickets of £350, and dance expenses of £300, then these can be put together as a dance profit in the income list. Note that it is quite all right to refer to profit in these

71

Receipts and Payments Account

Receipts		Payments	
Cash at bank	250	Dance expenses	70
Cash in hand	30	Electricity	97
Subscriptions	60	Postages	7
Sale of dance tickets	110	Insurance	50
Fund raising event	72		

Income and Expenditure Account

Income

Subscriptions		60	
Sale of dance tickets	110		
Less dance expenses	70		

Profit on dance		40	
Fund raising event		72	

			172

Expenditure

Electricity		97	
Postages		7	
Insurance		50	

			154

Surplus of income over expenditure			18

Fig. 22. Income and expenditure account.

Fig. 23. Receipts and payments account.

These are the figures of the Wolds Way Rambling Club:

Receipts and Payments Account

Subscriptions received	250	Fees for speaker	25
Income from coffee morning	65	Rent for Village Halls	35
Sale of rucksacks	350	Purchase of rucksacks	200
Takings from refreshments	15	Refreshments bought	7
Stock of tea, coffee etc at			
the start of the year	12	Stock of refreshments at	
		the end of the year	10

Prepare their Income and Expenditure Account.

cases.

In Figure 22 you can see how the receipts and payments account has been converted into an income and expenditure account.

Don't forget that you must always account for **prepayments** and **accruals**, just as in the profit and loss account.

It may sometimes be necessary to do a small trading account to ascertain how much of something was used during the period.

For example, supposing a table tennis club had a stock of table tennis balls of 500 at the start of the year, bought 350 during the year and had 300 left at the end. This would mean that they had used 550 during the year. You would want to charge 550 in the expenditure account for that year, even though only 350 had been bought: ie stock at start, plus purchases less stock at end.

Try this one

Take a look at Figure 23, and prepare their income and expenditure account.

Clubs also have balance sheets, just like any other organisation. You should have no problem with these by now. It is important to remember that anything paid in advance (by the club) is a current asset and money still owing (by the club) is a current liability.

An exam question

Below is an exam question from the London East Anglian Board, May 1989 paper 2, question 4.

On 1 January 1988 the Radcliffe Social Club had £890 in the bank. It had no other assets or liabilities. The following additional information is available during the year ended 31 December 1988.

Subscription received	
(of the above £150 is in advance for the next year)	3200
Rates on club house paid	670
New furniture purchases	
(£2500 has been paid, the balance is on credit,	
repayable within one year)	5000
Lighting and heating paid during the year	860
Receipts from admission to non-members for	
special shows	46000
Fees paid to performers at special shows	38500

On 31 December 1988 an electricity amount of £90 was unpaid.

a. Prepare for the year ended 31 December 1988:

    1. A receipts and payments account.

    2. An income and expenditure account.

b. Prepare a balance sheet as at 31 December 1988.

(25 marks)

Note
You will have to balance receipts and payments account like the cash book to arrive at bank/cash figure.

10
Accounts for Partnerships

Partnerships are formed for various reasons. The most obvious are:

1. A sharing of different areas of expertise, eg upholsterer and a carpenter may start making furniture together

2. To share the work load, especially to gain holidays or weekends. Doctors often form partnerships.

3. To gain more capital; one person may not have enough on their own.

What are the peculiarities of partnership accounts?

Capital
Each partner may put in a different amount of capital. It therefore seems fair to award interest on capital. This is usually done at the rate they would have got if they had invested the money in, say, a building society. A percentage rate is usually decided upon.

Salaries
These may or may not be paid to partners. If they are, it will probably be in proportion to the work done by them for the business.

Drawings
Just as a sole trader takes drawings, so may the partners. In a partnership it is usual to charge interest on these drawings. This is to discourage them from drawing too much money out of the business. As with interest on capital, a percentage rate is decided upon. It may be charged only for the months left in the financial year. Suppose the financial year is January to December, and a partner takes some drawings in August: he will be charged interest

for five months—August to December.

THE SLEEPING PARTNER

A **sleeping partner** is someone who invests money in the business, but also has **limited liability**. This means that if, say, he had invested £10000 and the business went bankrupt owing £400000, he would only be liable for his £10000—this is the maximum he could lose. The others would have to pay the rest of the debt even if this meant losing their homes and possessions. The sleeping partner, however, cannot take part in the management of the business. He has no say at all about how it is run.

DEED OF PARTNERSHIP

A partnership is often thought of as being two people, but in fact a business partnership may have between two and 20 people in it. When a partnership is formed, a **Deed of Partnership** is drawn up. This details various agreements about holidays, interest allowed on capital, interest charged on drawings and the ratio in which the profit is shared.

Under the **Partnership Act 1890** there are five rules which have to be followed in the event of there being no Deed of Partnership. This rarely happens, as it is obviously desirable to have a deed drawn up. The five rules are:

1. No salaries allowed.

2. No interest on drawings.

3. No interest on capitals.

4. If a partner puts in more than the agreed amount of capital then he will be paid 5 per cent interest *on the extra amount only*.

5. Partners equally share profits and losses.

APPROPRIATION ACCOUNT

The difference between the accounts of partnerships and sole traders is in the way the profit is shared, or appropriated, after the net profit figure is ascertained. This is done by drawing up an **appropriation account**. When this is done by itself, beginning with the net profit figure, the title is:

- Appropriation account for (names) for the year ended (date).

- If, however, you are drawing up the appropriation account along with the profit and loss account, then the title is:

- Profit and loss appropriation account for (names) for the year ended (date).

You do *not* put any titles in the middle of the accounts. Study the appropriation account drawn up from the following information.

The partnership of T.Dunne and B.Cowan

Net profit	20000
Salary for Cowan	5000
Interest on drawings:	
Dunne	500
Cowan	350
Interest on capital:	
Dunne	600
Cowan	400

Profit to be shared in the ratio of Dunne three-fifths, Cowan two-fifths. Figure 24 shows how it should be done.

Fig. 24. An appropriation account.

```
Appropriation account for Dunne and Cowan for the year ended
(date).
Net Profit                                          20,000
Add interest charged on drawings :
Dunne                                       500
Cowan                                       350
                                            ---        850
                                                   --------
                                                    20,850
Less salary for Cowan                     5,000
Less interest to be paid on capitals:
Dunne                               600
Cowan                               400
                                    ----  1,000
                                          ------      6,000
                                                   --------
                                                    14,850
Share of profits :
Dunne 3/5 (14850 divided by 5 then x 3)   8,910
Cowan 2/5                                  5,940
                                          -----     14,850
                                                   =======
```

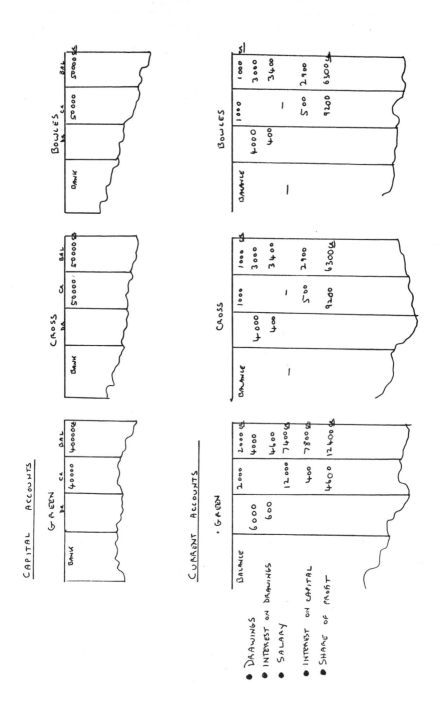

Fig. 25. Partnership capital and current accounts.

SUMMARY

● Anything to add on must be accounted for first.

● After everything else has been paid out, the remaining profit is shared in the agreed ratio.

Appropriation account exercise
Partnership appropriation account of Green, Cross and Bowles

Net profit	35000	
Interest on drawings:		
Green		600
Cross		400
Bowles		400
Salary for Green		12000
Interest on capital:		
Green		400
Cross		500
Bowles		500

Profit to be shared:
Cross and Bowles 40 per cent each.
Green 20 per cent.

CAPITAL ACCOUNTS AND CURRENT ACCOUNTS

When the owner of a business puts money into the business, a **capital account** is started. The capital account represents what the business owes to the owner. (This was explained in Chapter 2.)

All the amounts of interest on drawings, interest on capital and so on, must be entered on the capital account. In order to keep the capital accounts clear, a **current account** is opened for each partner. This must not be confused with the current account at the bank. The purpose of a partner's current account is to account for all the details which happen each year.

So each partner has a current account, as well as a capital account. The capital account remains fixed. It records the amount of capital which that partner put into the business, and remains the same. It is the current account which fluctuates with all the yearly happenings.

Suppose that Green, Cross and Bowles had each taken drawings of £6000, £4000 and £4000 respectively. Suppose also that their current accounts had credit balances of £2000, £1000 and £1000. If they had each put in capital of £40000, £50000 and £50000, their capital accounts would merely show this. Their capital and current accounts would appear as in Figure 25.

You will notice that, just as a capital account should have a credit balance, so should the current accounts. This represents what the business owes to the owner. If there is a debit balance, then the partner owes to the business.

An exam question
From London East Anglian Group, May 1989.

1. Explain the meaning of:
● drawings
● interest on drawings
● provision for depreciation
● working capital
● interest on capital.

2. Bunker and Lake are partners in a consultancy business. The following balances appear in their books at 31 December 1988 (after extraction of the trading and profit and loss accounts);

	£
Capital accounts (1 Jan 1988)	
Bunker	40000
Lake	50000
Current accounts (1 Jan 1988)	
Bunker	8400cr
Lake	4120dr
Drawings (for the year ended 31 December 1988)	
Bunker	24000
Lake	30000
Motor van at cost	12000
Provision for depreciation on motor van	9000
Premises	100000
Cash at bank	6596
Wages accrued	3936
Debtors	6420
Bank loan (repayable in 1990)	30000
Interest owing on bank loan	1200
Net trading profit	40600
Interest on drawings:	
Bunker	400
Lake	1800

The partners had agreed to allow 8 per cent per annum interest on capital and to share profits equally.

a. For the year ended 31 December 1988 prepare:
   i the profit and loss appropriation of the partnership.
   ii each partner's current account.
b. Prepare the balance sheet of the partnership as at 31 December 1988.

(25 marks)

11
Appropriation Accounts of Plc and Ltd

The last chapter examined the accounts of partnerships. You now know what a partnership is and how it works. Now you need to know:

- What does **plc** mean?
- What is **Ltd**?

Ltd means limited. It is the liability of the owners which is limited. Who are the owners? The owners are the people who own **shares** in the business. Suppose a partnership has become very large, with a lot of debts and many people owing money to it. If that partnership 'went bust', ie one of its creditors (usually a bank) calls for its money within a certain time and the business cannot pay it in that time, then the owners will be declared **bankrupt**. The business will be put into the hands of **receivers**, who will sell off all the assets to pay the creditors as much of the money owed to them as possible. This may include the personal belongings of the owners, such as their houses and cars.

LIMITED COMPANIES

Of course, there is a way to lessen this catastrophe. The business can become a **limited company**. This will mean that the owners' liability is limited to the amount of shares they own. If you owned £5000 worth of shares in your company, and it went bankrupt, you would only be expected to pay the £5000.

Private limited company
Ltd means **private limited company**. The issue of shares is to people whom you invite to buy them, not to the general public. The shares of private limited companies are often kept in the same family. If the business was previously a partnership, the partners

will probably become the share holders. A share is literally a share in the business. This is also a useful way of raising extra capital.

How do you register a private limited company?

Memorandum of Association
You have to send a **Memorandum of Association** to the **Registrar of Companies** in London. This must give:

- the name of the company;

- its address;

- the aims and objectives of the company;

- and the amount of money it would eventually like to raise through the sale of shares. This amount of money is called **authorised share capital**.

Articles of Association
You also have to send them your **Articles of Association**. These will be the details of:

- share holders

- voting rights

- the way the directors are appointed

- and details about **dividends**. Dividends are the share of profit given to shareholders each year, usually calculated as a percentage.

If these documents are approved, the registrar will issue a **certificate of incorporation**.

It is usual to ask a solicitor to draw up the documents for you, and this can be expensive. That is why some people buy **'off the peg' companies**—already formed, with a name.

Public limited company

Plc means public limited company. The shares are offered on the open market for anyone to buy. When someone has over 50 per cent of the shares, they are deemed to be in control of the company. Voting rights are linked to share ownership. When a public limited company is registered, it will be issued with a **trading certificate**, as well as the certificate of incorporation.

SUMMARY OF LIMITED COMPANIES

- Private limited company means shares sold by invitation only.

- Public limited company means that shares are sold on the open market, so someone else could gain control unless you keep more than 50 per cent yourself.

- Authorised share capital is the maximum amount which can be raised by issue of shares, as stated in the Memorandum of Association.

- Dividends are the share of profits given to shareholders each year.

WHAT SHOULD I KNOW ABOUT SHARES?

There are difference types of shares. A shareholder of **ordinary shares** will do well in years where the company makes a large profit, but in bad years they may not receive any dividend at all. This is decided by the directors.

The **preference share** is a safer investment. As the name suggests, they take preference over ordinary shares. They are paid out first, then the remainder is shared out to the ordinary shareholders. However, the preference share always carries a fixed percentage, and they will still be paid that percentage even when the ordinary shareholders may be getting more.

Share premium

Shares are issued at a certain cost (the **nominal value**). Sometimes a company can make a 'profit' by selling shares at more than their nominal value. Suppose a company issued 100 ordinary shares for £1 each. It then finds that it can sell another 50 at £1.50 each. The extra £25 it will have raised is called **share premium**. This share premium is used to fund dividends in bad years, or sometimes to fund a bonus issue of shares.

Bonus issue

A **bonus issue** is a free issue of shares to existing shareholders. This is usually based on the number of shares they hold. If they owned 100 shares, and the company was giving a bonus issue, they may be given something like one free share for every ten held. They would then be given ten free shares.

Issued share capital

This is the amount of money which has actually been raised from the sale of shares.

Called up capital

Sometimes a company may sell its shares in instalments. These are known as *calls*. A person may have decided to buy 100 £1 shares. He may pay the first call of £50 in January, and contract to pay the other £50 in June. In between these dates you would say that the **called up capital** was £50.

DEBENTURES

Another way for companies to raise money (capital) is by issuing **debentures**. A debenture really is a sort of i.o.u:

● The company owes the debenture holder the amount of money on the debenture;

● the company will have to pay interest to the debenture holders for the amount of money they are lending to them.

Debentures usually have a fixed term and a fixed amount of interest. If you have a ten-year, six per cent debenture which cost you £100, the company will have to pay you six per cent of that £100 for the next ten years. It will then have to give you your £100 back.

RESERVES

Sometimes the directors of a company will decide to transfer some of the profit to a **reserve fund**. It is always wise to try to build up reserves, as these can be used to fund new projects and promote growth of the company.

HOW DO YOU TREAT SHARES IN THE ACCOUNTS?

Suppose a company has an authorised share capital of £100000, divided into 25000 ten per cent preference shares of £1 each and 75000 ordinary shares of £1 each.

All the preference shares are issued and fully paid, but only 50000 of the ordinary shares are issued.

If the company made a good profit, paid the dividend on the preference shares and declared a dividend of nine per cent on the ordinary shares, how much money would be required for distribution?

There would be 25000 preference shares x 10 per cent = 2500
Add 50000 x 9 per cent   = 4500
                                                        ────
                                                        7000

Now try this one
N. Rose & Co
Another company, N. Rose and Co, has an authorised share capital
of £250000 divided into 100000 eight per cent preference shares
and 150000 ordinary shares. The issued capital is 75000 preference
shares and 100000 ordinary shares. It was decided to give 12 per
cent dividend on the ordinary shares. How much would be required
for distribution?

You must learn how this is shown in the accounts. Unlike the
partnership accounts, the appropriation accounts of plc and Ltd
companies often leave an unappropriated amount on the profit and
loss account to carry forward to the following year. This means
that when you start the appropriation account with net profit, you
must remember to add any unappropriated profit left from last
year.

An example of shares in the accounts
Brown Ltd had a balance of unappropriated profit of £5000. This
year the net profit was £2890. The authorised share capital was
£10000. Issued share capital was 3000 ten per cent preference
shares (£1 each) and 5000 ordinary shares (£1 each). The directors
decided to transfer £3000 to the general reserve. They recommended a dividend of eight per cent on the ordinary shares.

The appropriation account would look like this:

Unappropriated profit b/fwd	5000
Net profit	2890
	────
	7890
Transfer to general reserve	3000
	────
	4890
Preference dividend (10 per cent x 3000)	300
	────
	4590
Ordinary dividend (8 per cent x 5000)	400
	────
Unappropriated profit	4190

When writing a balance sheet, the 'financed by' section will now have to contain the details of the share capital. The authorised share capital must always be shown, but not added in. Therefore you show the authorised share capital and then underline it to show that you are not including it in your calculations. The issued share capital will be shown and accounted for. Note the example in Figure 26.

Note that proposed div. are current liabilities.

Fig. 26. Showing shares on the balance sheet.

```
Balance Sheet as at...

Fixed Assets                                         10000
Equipment

Current Assets
Stock                         5870
Debtors                      10834
Bank                          5700
Cash                           206
                             -----
                                         22610

Current liabilities
Creditors                    12000
Proposed dividends             700
                             ------
                                         12700
                                         -----
                                                      9910
                                                     -----
                                                     19910
                                                     -----

Financed by
                                                     10000
Authorised share capital                             =====

Issued share capital:
Preference shares             3000
Ordinary shares              5000
                             ----
                                                      8000
                             7720
General reserve              4190
Unappropriated profit        ----
                                                     11910
                                                     -----
                                                     19910
                                                     -----
```

An exam question
Now try to answer the following question from the NEA Summer exam 1991 (paper 2 question 2).

From the information given below you are required to prepare for Streamline plc:

a. a profit and loss appropriation account for the year ended 31 December 1990;

b. a balance sheet as at 31 December 1990.

Streamline plc has an authorised share capital of £520000, divided into 500000 £1 ordinary shares and 20000 5 per cent preference shares of £1 each. Of these shares, 300000 ordinary shares and all of the 5 per cent preference shares have been issued and are fully paid.

In addition to the above information, the following balances remained in the accounts after the profit and loss account had been prepared for the year ended 31 December 1990:

	Dr	Cr
Plant and machinery at cost	140000	
Provision for depreciation on plant and machinery		50000
Premises at cost	250000	
Profit and loss account balance (1 January 1990)		34000
Net trading profit for year ended 31 December 1990		15000
Wages owing		3900
Bank balance	15280	
Stock (31 December 1990)	16540	
Trade debtors and creditors	12080	3000
Advertising prepaid	2000	
General reserve		10000

The directors have proposed the payment of the preference share dividend, and an ordinary share dividend of six per cent. They also recommend a transfer of £20000 to the general reserve.

(Marks a = 9; b = 37)

12
Interpretation of Final Accounts

The whole purpose of **final accounts** is to assess how well the business is performing. The profit and loss account tells you how much profit you have made. The balance sheet tells you how the business stands at a particuar date. However, before you begin to look at the final accounts, it would be as well to remind yourself of their limitations.

WORKING OUT PROFIT

The profit shown by the profit and loss account bears no relation to the amount of money you actually have in the bank. This is because of the following:

- Stock. The stock figures used are based upon the firm's method of valuation of its stock (see note at end of chapter). They also depend on the accuracy of the stocktaking.

- Depreciation. Depreciation is based upon estimated values.

- Doubtful debts. The provision for doubtful debts is only an estimated figure.

- These three points are variable; a different accountant may arrive at a different profit figure. This seems a difficult concept to grasp. Most people believe that only one answer could be correct, but this is not so.

Fixed assets
The cost of the asset is a known and definite figure, but the depreciation is an estimated figure. Therefore the net figure used is an estimated figure.

Current assets
Stock could vary as stated under profit.

Debtors figure takes into account doubtful debts which are an estimated figure.

Interpreting the final accounts
In spite of all these variables, you *can* interpret the final accounts and obtain a fair view of the state of the business. Suppose you were considering investing in a company. Consider the balance sheet like this:

Fixed assets
• Is the depreciation realistic?

• Are new assets being purchased? Are old ones being written off? (Or depreciated to nothing?)

• Are there plenty of worthwhile assets? (Do they own the premises?)

Current assets
• Is there a sensible balance between stock, debtors, bank and cash? Beware too high a debtors figure (except in the case of a firm making Easter eggs, which may have a high debtors figure and low stock just after Easter!).

• Is the stock figure too high: too much money tied up in it? Or too low: orders could be lost through delay. Could be low due to lack of funds.

• Is the debtors figure increasing. If so, is there a corresponding increase in sales? Are bad debts increasing? Should better discounts be offered to encourage prompt payment?

• Bank/cash: is there a large balance? If so should this be employed elsewhere? On the other hand, shortages mean that you can't buy in great bulk and obtain good discounts, etc.

• Creditors: Are they increasing? Is this because of shortage of funds? It could be due to heavy buying just before a peak period, eg Christmas, or that the firm is trying to expand. You would want to find out if they had been outstanding for very long and if they were pressing for payment.

● Are reserves being built up? Is profit being put back into the business? How much does the company owe in long-term loans?

USING RATIOS

To analyse even further, the following ratios can be used.

To test for efficiency

Return on capital employed $=$ profit x 100

$$\text{capital employed}$$

Note: **capital employed** is the capital figure used in the balance sheet, ie owner's capital, partners' capital accounts or issued share capital, depending on the type of business. (This figure should not include long-term loans.)

Gross profit ratio $=$ gross profit x 100

$$\text{sales}$$

Net Profit ratio $=$ net profit x 100

$$\text{sales}$$

Working capital $=$ current assets less current liabilities.

To test for solvency

Current ratio $=$ current assets

$$\text{current liabilities}$$

(Ideal is 2:1 - that is, CA:CL.)

Acid test (or quick asset) ratio $=$ current assets less stock

$$\text{current liabilities}$$

Rate of stock turnover $=$ Cost of sales

$$\text{average stock}$$

To calculate capital

Owners capital/shareholders funds =

- capital at start + net profit less drawings;

- or, capital accounts + current accounts;

- or, issued shares + reserves.

Which one of those three methods is used, of course, depends on the type of business: sole trader, partnership or limited company.

It will be necessary to learn all these ratios, as you may be expected to use them in exam questions.

An exam question

The following is taken from the NEA 1988 exam paper. Try it and then check your answers with those at the back of the book.

On 31 May 1988 Fiona Maxwell presents you with copies of balance sheets of two engineering firms. She says that she is thinking of expanding her light engineering business by taking over one of these firms and she asks you for advice. The balance sheets are shown below.

Metal Products Ltd balance sheet as at 30 September 1987

	£
Premises, at cost	15000
Machinery, at cost	5000
Stock, at cost (market value £3000)	2000
Debtors	1800
Bank balance	200
	24000
Share capital: authorisd and issued	19360
Undistributed profits	2640
Creditors	2000
	24000

Forge Engineering Ltd balance sheet as at 30 June 1987

	£	£
Premises, at cost		35000
Machinery, at cost, less depreciation		15000
Stock, at cost (market value £12000)		20000
Debtors	9000	
Less provision for doubtful debts	1000	8000
		78000
Share capital: authorised and issued		63800
Undistributed profits		4200
Creditors		8000
Bank overdraft		2000
		78000

Using a lined answer sheet, prepare a report which should include the following points:

a. A criticism of the information shown in the balance sheets. (8 marks.)

b. An explanation of additional accounting information which is required. (6 marks.)

c. Any calculations you think would be useful. (9 marks.)

d. A recommendation as to whether either firm should be taken over, giving your reasons. (6 marks.)

Note that criticism in this question does not mean a criticism of the layout, but rather an appraisal of the contents.

STOCK VALUATION

As mentioned earlier in the book, stock is always valued at cost price (or selling price if it is lower). However, it is not always so easy to work this out. Suppose you have a box full of brass screws. You have bought some at four pence each. A month later, you buy some more at six pence each. You keep them all in the same box. It is not always easy to know which cost four pence and which cost six pence. You will not wish to label every screw!

There are three ways of costing your screws:

- **FIFO**, first in, first out

- **LIFO**, last in first out

- and **AVCO**, average cost.

With FIFO you assume that the first screws you take out cost four pence (you will know how many of each you should have).

With LIFO you assume that the first ones you take out cost six pence.

With AVCO you assume that all the screws cost five pence (4 + 6 divided by 2).

Obviously, the value of your stock would depend on which of these methods you are using. You must use the same method each year, applying the consistency concept.

13
Funds Flow Statements

There is another method of interpretation of final accounts, which is effective if you have access to two years' accounts for comparison. It is called a **funds flow statement** and consists of two lists:

- sources of funds
- application of funds.

These are compiled from the increases or decreases of the various components of the balance sheet.

SOURCES OF FUNDS

A fairly obvious source of funds is an increase in a loan.

Another obvious source is the net profit for the year.

Much less obvious is that an increase in creditors is a source of funds. This is because you have gained something from the creditors without (yet) paying for it.

APPLICATION OF FUNDS

An increase in fixed assets would be an application of funds, as this must mean that new assets have been purchased.

An increase in stock would be an application of funds, as you must have spent some money on more stock.

An increase in debtors is less obvious. You have had the expense of outlay without yet receiving any recompense, so this is an application of funds.

Drawings are an application too of course.

WORKING IT OUT

It is all very logical, but needs some thought. Some people understand this immediately, while others always have to argue

with themselves. Don't worry if you are one of the latter. You are
certainly not alone.

Look at the two balance sheets of G.Bunter in Figure 27.

Now you can do your flow of funds statement. This is sometimes
called a **sources and applications of funds statement**.

Look at Figure 28. Note that the statement is labelled as at the
date of the second year. Obviously you could not do this after the
first year! This is why the profit figure used is that of the second
year. Also the drawings figure is that of the second year.

Fig. 27. Preparation for flow of funds statement.

BALANCE SHEETS OF G.BUNTER

	Year 1		Year 2	
Fixed Assets		5 000		6120
Current Assets				
Stock	3 750		4250	
Debtors	2 890		3 450	
Bank	280		2 040	
		6920		9 740
Current Liabilities				
Creditors	2725		2 950	
		4195		6 790
		9 195		12 910
Financed By:-				
Capital at start	6745		9 195	
Less Drawings	1 000		2 000	
		5 745		7195
Add Net Profit		3450		5 715
		9 195		12 910

Flow of Funds Statement for G.Bunter as at (date of Yr. 2)

Sources of Funds

Net Profit	5715
Increase in Creditors	225
	5940

Application of Funds

Increase in Fixed Assets	1120	
" " Debtors	560	
" " Stock	500	
Drawings	2000	
		4180
Excess of Sources over Applications		1760

Proof

Bank at Start	280	
Bank at End	2040	
Increase in Bank	(1760)	

Fig. 28. Flow of funds statement.

SUMMARY AND PRACTICE

● Increase in fixed assets must mean that money has been spent buying new assets. Therefore this is an application of funds.

● The same applies to increase in stock.

● The increase in debtors is an application of funds because you have had to spend in order to supply, and have not yet been paid.

● The drawings is an obvious application.

- Decrease in creditors means you have spent money to pay some of them off, so it is an application.

- Note that the difference in cash and bank in year one and year two proves that your statement is correct.

Examples to try
Now try some examples yourself (see figs. 29 and 30). You will find the answers in the back of the book.

Fig. 29. Practice sheet for flow of funds statement (1).

BALANCE SHEETS OF KS ALARMS

	YEAR 1		YEAR 2	
FIXED ASSETS		30,000		50,000
CURRENT ASSETS				
STOCK	7,000		12,000	
DEBTORS	3,500		6,000	
BANK	12,000		5,000	
	22,500		23,000	
CURRENT LIABILITIES				
CREDITORS	3,700		10,500	
		18,800		12,500
		48,800		62,500
FINANCED BY:				
CAPITAL AT START		40,000		48,800
+ NET PROFIT		8,800		9,700
LOAN		—		4,000
		48,800		62,500

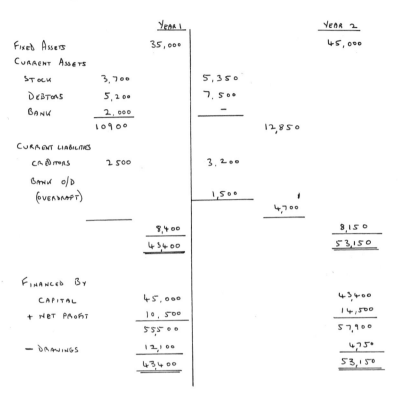

Balance Sheets of J. Bird

	Year 1		Year 2
Fixed Assets	35,000		45,000
Current Assets			
Stock	3,700	5,350	
Debtors	5,200	7,500	
Bank	2,000	—	
	10900		12,850
Current Liabilities			
Creditors	2500	3,200	
Bank o/d (overdraft)		1,500	
			4,700
	8,400		8,150
	43,400		53,150
Financed By			
Capital	45,000		43,400
+ Net Profit	10,500		14,500
	55500		57,900
− Drawings	12,100		4750
	43,400		53,150

Fig. 30. Practice sheet for flow of funds statement (2).

14
What to Do With Incomplete Records

Many businesses do not keep complete accounting records. They may have a cash book. Some small firms just put all paperwork on one side in a file. Sometimes everything is impaled on a spike in a block of wood, for safe keeping until someone has time to do something about it.

It is very costly to ask an accountant to come and sort that lot out. A freelance book-keeper can find him/herself very much in demand. Therefore you should find this chapter especially useful in your future work, as well as for the exam.

You must collect as much information as you can: till receipts, cheque book stubs, general receipts and so on. Now, from this heap of assorted 'evidence' you must try to write up some correct accounts.

Darren Thompson has been trading for a year now. He sells computer software from a small shop which has been lent to him rent-free for two years. When he started he had saved up £1500 and was given another £500 to help him get started. He bought some shelving for £500. His starting stock of software cost him £2000 and he was able to buy this on credit from Skyway Products. He bought a second-hand till for £350.

Now, after one year's trading, you can gather the following information:

- money taken over the counter had amounted to £10000;
- he had paid his creditors (Skyway Products) a total of £5000;
- running expenses such as electricity and telephone came to £649;
- money owing to Skyway was £1560;
- Darren had taken out £1500 in drawings;
- his stock was now worth £1975.

STATEMENT OF AFFAIRS

The first thing you must do is to prepare a **statement of affairs** as at the starting date. This is a very basic sort of balance sheet. Darren's would look like this:

Till	350
Stock	2000
Shelves	500
Cash (after buying above)	1150
	4000
Creditor	
Skyway Products	2000
Net worth (capital)	2000

PREPARING THE TRADING AND PROFIT AND LOSS ACCOUNTS

You need to find the figures for sales and purchases so that you can prepare the trading and profit and loss accounts.

To find the sales figure

In Darren's case this is easy: it is his takings of £10000.

If he had been selling things on credit, you would have:

- taken the figure received from debtors
- deducted debtors at start of year;
- then added debtors at end of year.

This would have given you the true figure for *this* year. Debtors at start would belong to last year's account, debtors at end to this year.

To find the purchases figure

Use the same principle.

The cash paid to creditors was	5000
Less owing at start	2000
	3000
Add owing at end	1560
Purchases for year =	4560

The trading and profit and loss account

You are now ready to do this.

Sales		10000
Stock at start	2000	
Add purchases	4560	
	———	
	6560	
Less closing stock	1975	
	———	
		4585
		———
Gross profit		5415
Expenses		649
		———
Net profit		4766
		———

Before you can do the balance sheet, you will have to check that the cash he has (either in hand or at the bank) is exactly the amount it should be. Just do a simple cash book, as in Figure 31.

Fig. 31. Cash book.

CASH BOOK				
BALANCE AT START	1150	CASH PAID TO CREDITOR	5000
RECEIVED FROM CASH SALES	10000	EXPENSES	649
		DRAWINGS	1500
		BALANCE TO C/D	4001
	11150		11150
BALANCE B/D	4001		

The balance sheet
Now the balance sheet can be set out.

Balance sheet for Darren Thompson as at (date)

Fixed assets			
Till			350
Shelves			500
			850
Current Assets			
Stock	1975		
Cash	4001		
		5976	
Current liabilities			
Creditor	1560		
Working capital			4416
			5266
Financed by			
Capital at start			2000
Add net profit			4766
			6766
Less drawings			1500
			5266

SUMMARY AND PRACTICE

- First gather as much information as possible.
- Next, get your starting point; do the statement of affairs.
- Now, begin to work through the final accounts for the year, working out some of the figures as you go.

It is not so difficult to achieve a full set of accounts providing that you have all the necessary basic information. There are times, of course, when you really have to estimate. A trader may not have a till which gives a print-out. He may have taken drawings and not recorded it. He may have paid expenses out of the till, or taken goods from stock for his own use. This taking of stock is classed as drawings. It should be deducted from purchases in the trading account, as it reduces the amount of purchases used for the business.

Of course, if you are trying to sort out the book-keeping as well as the final accounts, you will have a tougher job. Persistence is the key. You will have to find out who owes the business money. The creditors will soon contact you! With any luck, your business-man will have kept some record of money owing to him, even if it seems rather primitive to you. Just methodically sort through the 'evidence', putting it in date order first. Then you will have to ascertain who has paid their bills.

Unfortunately, sometimes people will pay their bills in the pub over a pint of beer or two. This way, your businessman will probably have used the proceeds. This is where tact and diplomacy are useful assets. Out of necessity, you will soon acquire the skills to winkle out unpaid bills and not harass those who have paid. However, luckily this will not apply to GCSE exam questions. It is merely a little underpinning to balance the knowledge you are quickly attaining.

Alfred Smith's business

As always, the only way to check that you have really understood these methods is to actually work one out.

The following information has been gathered about the business of Alfred Smith for the month of March:

Cash received from customers	53
Invoices sent for work completed:	
Mrs Jones	254
Mrs Ginn	110
Mr Glew	235
Mr Thompson	145
Expenses paid out:	
Materials	352
Overheads	178
Cash in bank on 1 March	976
Stock of unused materials at end of month	350
Stock of materials at start of month	490

Prepare a trading and profit and loss account and a balance sheet for Alfred for the month.

15
Mark Up and Margin

You will need to understand the relationship between **mark up** and **margin**. It is really quite simple: if you were to buy an article for say £8, and then sell it again for £12, the mark up and margin are both £4. However, the mark up is one half of the cost price but the margin, still £4, is a third of the selling price (see Figure 32).

HOW DOES THIS APPLY TO ACCOUNTS?

Look at this trading account

Sales		3600
Stock at start	1000	
Purchases	2800	
	3800	
Stock at end	1400	
Cost of sales		2400
Gross profit		1200

- What is the margin?

- What is the mark up?

The margin is one third, or 33 1/3 per cent.

$$\frac{\text{Gross profit}}{\text{Sales}} = \frac{1200}{3600}$$

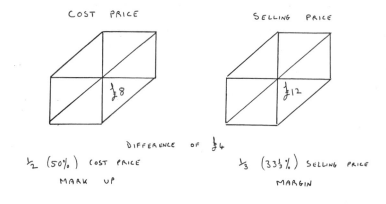

Fig. 32. Mark up and margin.

Similarly the mark up is one half or 50 per cent.

$$\text{Mark up} = \frac{\text{Gross profit}}{\text{Cost of sales}} = \frac{1200}{2400}$$

Another trading account

Sales	22000
Opening stock	1700
Purchases	17000
	18700
Closing stock	2200
Cost of sales	16500
Gross profit	5500

- What is the mark up and margin?
- What is the average stock?
- What is the turnover?

The mark up is one third. The margin is one quarter.
   Note: These combinations always go together:
   Mark up one third; margin quarter
   Mark up half; margin one third
   Mark up quarter; margin one fifth

Average stock is the two stock figures added together, then divided by two. **Turnover** is just another word for sales.

So the average stock is 1950 and the turnover is 22000.

SUMMARY AND PRACTICE

- The combinations of mark up and margin always follow the same pattern, as described above.

- Mark up is calculated on cost price; margin on selling price.

Will Grant's account
Will Grant's mark up is 50 per cent.

Average stock	3400
Purchases	2600
Opening stock	3200

Find out:
1. Closing stock
2. Gross profit
3. Sales

Hint: draw up a skeleton trading account and work backwards, filling in the blanks. The questions are in the order you'll need to progress. Answer at the back of the book, but try to do it first!

An exam question from the NEA 1989 paper.
Owing to pressure of work, Mr Singh postponed his stocktaking to Sunday 4 June 1989, although his financial year ended on 31 May 1989.

At 4 June he valued his stock at £7600 (cost price).

In the period 1—4 June:

Purchases were £840.
Takings at tills £820.
Customer returned goods originally sold to him for £60.
Goods sold on credit amounted to £280.
Mr Singh took goods £30 cost price for own use.
His gross profit is 25 per cent of cost.

Calculate the amount of stock at 31 May which should be shown in his trading account to 31 May 1989. Show all workings.

16
How to Do a Bank Reconciliation

You now need to refer back to the cash book. This will be useful revision at this stage.

In addition to your cash book, you will have a further check on your cash position via statements from the bank. The bank statement will have the income and outgoings the opposite way round from your cash book.

It is also very likely that the balance on the statement will differ from that in the cash book. This is due to:

- **Unpresented cheques**: cheques paid to people but not yet appearing on the bank statement.

- **Charges** made by the bank (unknown to you until now and therefore not entered in the cash book).

- **Dishonoured cheques**. Sometimes you will have received a cheque, paid it into the bank and had it returned to you marked 'Refer to drawer' (the drawer is the person who is paying). This means that either there are insufficient funds in their account to cover the cheque, or there is a fault in the way the cheque was made out. The date could be in the future (post-dated) or out of date (usually more than six months). The signature could be missing or incorrect, or perhaps the amount in words does not tally with the amount in figures.

You therefore have to reconcile the cash book to the bank statement, to check that your figures are correct and to obtain your true cash position.

DIFFERENT METHODS YOU CAN USE

There are three ways to do this process:

● reconcile the cash book total to the bank statement;

● reconcile the bank statement to the cash book;

● obtain a corrected total for both which agrees.

The third method is the most common, and is the one used here. First work out the corrected cash book total. Then also work out a corrected total for the bank statement. In other words, you begin with the cash book total and put on to it all the things on the bank statement that it does not contain. Then you start again with the bank statement total and put on it all the things in the cash book that are not on it.

Fig. 33. Reconciling cash book to bank statement.

CASH BOOK

DETAILS	BANK	DETAILS	BANK
BALANCE B/Fwd	100.00		
S. SMITH	50.00	D. BATES	200.00
P. DAVIES	20.00	R. BATTY	59.00
R. SINCLAIR	152.00	G. CRESSWELL	19.00
B. PETTY	47.00	M.D.T. SERVICES	25.00
CASH PAID INTO BANK	50.00		
J. JOHNSON	56.00		
		BALANCE TO c/d	172.00
	475.00		475.00
B/Fwd	172.00		

Bank Statement

			100.00 CB
Balance			
Cash		50.00	
Cheque		50.00	
Cheque		20.00	
Cheque	200.00		20.00 CA
Cheque dishnd	152.00	152.00	
Cheque		47.00	
Charges	10.00		57.00cr.

An example

Take a look at Figure 33.

You begin with the total of the bank column in the cash book: £172.00

Less bank charges	10.00	
Less: dishonoured cheque	152.00	
	———	162.00
Corrected balance		10.00

Balance as per bank statement:		
		57.00
Add cheque from J.Johnson		56.00
		———
		113.00
Less cheques paid out	59.00	
(Not yet recorded by bank)	19.00	
	25.00	
	———	103.00
		———
		10.00

In each case you have taken the current balance and added or deducted items which have not yet been processed through your system. You have now arrived at the same balance for both.

On the cash book you had to deduct bank charges. These have not yet appeared in your cash book because you did not know of them. They will subsequently be entered in the credit (out) side of the cash book. You also deducted the dishonoured cheque, which was previously entered in the cash book on the debit (in) side. Now that you won't be getting the money after all, it will eventually have to be entered into your cash book on the credit side to take it out again. In the meantime, you are just doing the reconciliation, so deduct it from your cash book total.

Try the following

Do a reconciliation based on the cash book and bank statement in Figure 34.

If you have a bank account, you could further practise by keeping a simple cash book of your personal expenses, then reconcile this with your bank statement.

CASH BOOK

DETAILS	BANK		DETAILS	BANK
BALANCE B/Fwd.	138·00			
S. NAISMITH	100·00		L. FRANCIS	98·00
P. SMITH	9·00		F. BRIGGS	92·00
K. PETTY	106·00		D. BROWN	20·00
C. ASHTON	92·00		J. THOMPSON	32·00
CASH PAID INTO BANK	50·00			
G. ROBIN	62·00			
			BALANCE TO c/Fwd.	315·00
	557·00			557·00
BALANCE B/Fwd	315·00			

Bank Statement

Balance			138.00 CR
Cheque		100.00	247.00
Cheque		9.00	149.00
Cheque	98.00		57.00
Cheque	92.00		107.00
Cash		50.00	
Standing order		37.00	144.00
Cheque	20.00		124.00
Charges	10.00		114.00 CR

Fig. 34. Exercise in reconciling.

An exam question

Now do the exam question shown in Figure 35 from the Northern Ireland Schools Examination Council 1988 (paper 2 question 2).

Also answer this exam question. (The first part was included in the first chapter.)

- At the end of each month why will the cash book 'bank' balance differ from that appearing in the bank statement covering the same period? Give *four* reasons.

2. This is the bank account for the month of April of Jane who runs a small business.

Dr.		Jane's Bank Account				Cr.
Apr 3	Balance b/f	642·87	Apr 8	R. M. Jones	56·31	
3	Sales	267·31	8	Smith Stores Ltd	12·67	
28	Sales	189·43	8	M. Maguire	315·74	
31	Sales	210·50	8	L. Kelly	123·54	
			15	M. R. Morgan	117·84	
			15	Johnston & Black Ltd	159·74	
			31	Balance	524·27	
		£1310·11			£1310·11	
May 1	Balance b/f	524·27				

Below is Jane's Bank Statement for April

JANE JOHNSTON
67 MARKET STREET
CASTLETOWN

IN ACCOUNT WITH
PROVINCE-WIDE BANK
WEST STREET
CASTLETOWN

Account No. 025 673 216

DATE	PARTICULARS	DEBIT	CREDIT	BALANCE
1988				
1	Balance forward			642·87
3	LTG		267·31	910·18
8	824	56·31		853·87
11	827	123·54		730·33
17	CT		26·89	757·22
19	826	315·74		441·48
20	828	117·84		323·64
21	SO	93·56		230·08
26	829	159·74		70·34
28	LTG		189·43	259·77
31	CG	18·50		241·27

DD	Direct Debit	CT	Credit Transfer	DR	Overdrawn Balance
CD	Cash Dispenser	CG	Charges	SO	Standing Order

Study both records of Jane's bank account and answer the questions which follow.

(i) Give Jane *three* reasons why her Bank Statement balance and the balance from her own bank account are not the same.

(a) ....

(b) ....

(c) .... **(6)**

(ii) Explain to Jane why the cheque numbers do not appear in the Bank Statement in the same order as they appear in her own record.

....

.... **(4)**

(iii) Use Jane's Bank Account on the opposite page to make any necessary entries to bring it up to date. **(6)**

(iv) In the space below prepare a Bank Reconciliation Statement. **(10)**

Fig. 35. Reconciliation exam question.

17
Working with Petty Cash

It is often necessary to deal with very small amounts of money. This includes cash to buy tea or coffee for use at work, bus fares and other expenses which should be charged to the business. The cash book could quickly become very complicated with all these minor amounts entered in it. The answer is to have a separate cash book for the minor transactions. This is knows as a **petty cash book**.

IMPREST

Most firms operate their petty cash using what is known as the **imprest** system (even if they don't call it that!). Imprest simply means **float**. Periodically, perhaps weekly or monthly, the person in charge of petty cash will be given a float. This is an amount of money.

PETTY CASH VOUCHERS

The petty cashier will also be given a pad of **petty cash vouchers**. Whenever the cashier issues anyone with some petty cash, a voucher is completed, signed by the recipient and kept in the petty cash box. This means that, at any time, the totals of the actual cash plus the amounts on the vouchers should equal the amount of the original float.

For example, suppose that you are in charge of the petty cash. You are given £50 float on the first of the month. During the month, someone asks you for £5 to buy some coffee and sugar. You write the details on the voucher and the person signs it. (See Figure 36.) You will give the person the £5 and put the voucher in the cash box. Note that in the space marked **folio**, you will begin your own numbering system.

If you now add up the cash you have left, you should have £45 plus a voucher for £5, which agrees with the original float of £50.

Petty cash

Signature	Passed by	Folio number
B. Jones		1

Date	Description	Job no	Amount	
1-10-91	Cash to buy coffee + sugar	-	5	—
		Total	5	—

Fig. 36. Petty cash voucher.

You can see that throughout the week/month there will be many transactions, and this system is a useful check on the cash.

THE PETTY CASH BOOK

Of course, these transactions are also recorded elsewhere. A special cash book is kept, called the petty cash book. Figure 37 shows an example. The float is entered on the left, and all the transactions are analysed into the columns on the right. Your folio numbers are used here to identify the vouchers.

As an example enter up the petty cash book of Wold Green Florists. During the month of March, their petty cash transactions were as follows:

1 March Received imprest (float) of £50.
2 March Paid out £5 for coffee and sugar.
4 March Paid window cleaner £6.50.
7 March Paid out bus fares of £2.
10 March Bought stamps £11.
15 March Paid out £6 for cleaning materials.
20 March Paid out £10 petrol money for firm's mini bus.
25 March Paid out £2 for milk powder.
30 March Paid window cleaner £6.50 (again).

The petty cash book will appear as in Figure 38. The petty cashier will now be given sufficient money to restore the float (imprest).

Now continue it yourself:

FLOAT RECEIVED	DATE	DETAILS	VOUCHER No.	TOTAL	POSTAGES	OFFICE SUNDRIES	CLEANING	STATIONERY	TRAVELLING EXPENSES	

Fig. 37. Petty cash book (above).
Fig. 38. Petty cash book example (below).

FLOAT RECEIVED	DATE	DETAILS	VOUCHER No.	TOTAL	POSTAGES	OFFICE SUNDRIES	CLEANING	STATIONERY	TRAVELLING EXPENSES	
50.00	MARCH 1	BANK								
	2	COFFEE + SUGAR	1	5.00		5.00				
	4	WINDOW CLEANER	2	6.50			6.50			
	7	BUS FARES	3	2.00					2.00	
	10	STAMPS	4	11.00	11.00					
	15	CLEANING MATS	5	6.00			6.00			
	20	PETROL	6	10.00					10.00	
	25	MILK POWDER	7	2.00		2.00				
	30	WINDOW CLEANER	8	6.50			6.50			
				49.00	11.00	7.00	19.00		12.00	
		BAL TO c/d		1.00						
50.00				50.00						
1.00		BAL B/d								
49.00		BANK								

115

1 April Received money to restore the imprest.
4 April Paid out £4.50 for coffee.
7 April Paid window cleaner £6.50.
10 April Bought stamps £11.
15 April Bought a new pad of petty cash vouchers £0.50.
20 April Paid out bus fares £2.75.
24 April Paid out £5 for biscuits for seminar.
30 April Paid window cleaner £6.50.

How much impress will you need?

An exam question
The question set in Figure 39 is from the Northern Ireland Schools
Examination Council (paper 1) Summer 1989.

SUMMARY

- The petty cash system is designed to take care of the many small cash transactions of a business.

- The imprest is the float, or amount of money given to the petty cashier periodically.

- The totals on the petty cash vouchers plus the cash in the box should always equal the amount of the original float.

- All petty cash transactions are recorded in the petty cash book.

12. Brian Jones is in charge of the Petty Cash in his firm. The Petty Cash is run on the Imprest System with the amount being made up on the Friday afternoon each week. At the start of each week he has £25 in his cash box.

   (a) What proof does the firm have that Brian actually pays out the amounts entered in the Petty Cash Book and is not just putting the money in his own pocket?

   ....

   ....

   (b) Write up the Petty Cash Book for the week beginning 8 September from the details given above and the vouchers below.

   (c) Make the necessary entries to show how the Petty Cash Book is completed and balanced on the Friday afternoon.   (31)

PETTY CASH		
Voucher No. 85 Date 8 Sept	£	p
Bus Fares City Centre	–	60
Total	–	60
Received by J Smith		

PETTY CASH		
Voucher No. 88 Date 10 Sept	£	p
Taxi to station Sale Manager	3	–
Total	3	–
Received by RL		

PETTY CASH		
Voucher No. 86 Date 5 Sept	£	p
2nd class stamps Parcel	1 2	30 10
Total	3	40
Received by T Orr		

PETTY CASH		
Voucher No. 89 Date 10 Sept	£	p
Rail Fare Coleraine	10	–
Total	10	–
Received by JMB		

PETTY CASH		
Voucher No. 87 Date 9 Sept	£	p
Window cleaner	4	–
Total	4	–
Received by Pat Harrison		

PETTY CASH		
Voucher No. 90 Date 12 Sept	£	p
Stamps	2	10
Total	2	10
Received by T Orr		

[Turn over

Fig. 39. Petty cash exam question.

12.

PETTY CASH BOOK							
Receipts	Date	Details	Voucher Number	Total Payments	Cleaning	Postage	Travelling Expenses

PETTY CASH BOOK							
Receipts	Date	Details	Voucher Number	Total Payments	Cleaning	Postage	Travelling Expenses

8

Fig. 39. continued.

18
Break Even Analysis

Some GCSE syllabuses do not include this topic. Check with your teacher or centre. As with the next chapter, you will eventually have to cover this if you intend to go on to do the GCE 'A' level.

BREAK EVEN POINT

As its name suggests, **break even analysis** simply involves finding the point at which the business will break even. This means finding out what volume of sales is needed for the business to be in neither profit nor loss. The way to calculate this is to find out:

- the total fixed costs
- the variable costs per unit (item) sold
- the number of items sold and selling price

As an example, suppose that Shirley Minton makes teddy bears. Her fixed costs are £10000. Her selling price is £8 per teddy bear. The variable costs per teddy bear are £3 each. This variation could be due to such things as staff on piece-work or fluctuating costs of materials. She expects to sell 10000 teddy bears. Shirley's break even point would be:

$$\frac{\text{Total fixed costs}}{\text{Selling price—variable cost}} = \frac{10000}{8-3}$$

The answer is 2000 units (teddy bears).

This means that Shirley must sell 2000 teddy bears just to break even. To make a profit she must make more. This can be illustrated in a graph, shown in Figure 40.

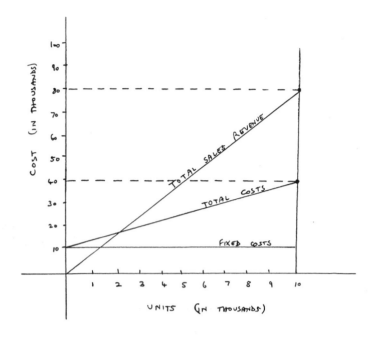

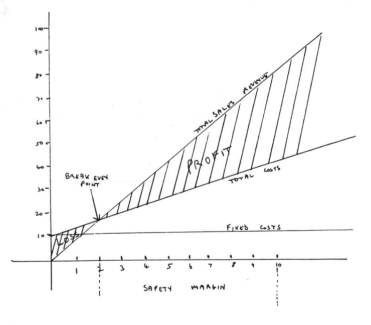

Fig. 40. Break even chart. Note the labels of the different parts of the graph. The safety margin is from break even point to expected sales.

To plot sales revenue
Expected sales x selling price = 80,000.
Plot from 10,000 (expected sales) to 80,000.
Draw a line from 0 to this point.

To plot total costs
Variable costs x expected sales + fixed costs = 10,000 x 3 + 10,000 = 40,000.
Plot from 10,000 (expected sales) to 40,000.
Draw a line from fixed costs (10,000) to this point.

Finding the break even point
The point where the two lines cross is break even point.

The graph is a very useful visual indication of a business's progress. Notice the names of the different lines and parts of the graph.

Now try this
Do a formula and a graph based on the information that Jason Rose produced about his business:

Total fixed costs £12000
Selling price per unit £10
Variable costs per unit £4
Expected sales 8000

An exam question
The question in Figure 41 is from the Northern Ireland Schools Examination Council 1989 (paper 3 question 3, parts a-d).

3. Arnold has begun manufacturing computer desks and has presented you with the following information regarding his business for the year:

Direct Labour costs	£4 per desk
Raw Material costs	£12 per desk
Fixed Expenses	£1,000 per year
Selling price	£20 per desk

Anticipated units produced and sold during the year: 500.

REQUIRED

(a) Draw a 'break-even graph' to illustrate Arnold's:

      break-even point
      fixed costs
      total costs
      sales revenue
      area of loss
      margin of safety.   **(28)**

(b) How many desks must he produce and sell in order to break-even?

....   **(2)**

(c) Assuming fixed costs and variable costs remain the same describe the effect of an increase in sales on the break-even point and area of profit.

....
....
....   **(6)**

(d) By using calculations or by using your graph, show the effect of variable costs increasing by 12.5%. Indicate clearly:

    (i) how many units would have to be produced and sold to break-even,
    (ii) the sales revenue at break-even.

....   **(8)**

12

Fig. 41. Break even exam question.

19
Cash Budgets

Do not confuse a **cash budget** with the flow of funds/sources and application of funds described in Chapter 13. Some people call the flow of funds statement a cash flow statement, and this could be confusing. Here you are only concerned with the cash *budget*.

Some GCSE syllabuses do not include this topic. Check with your teacher or centre. However, if you intend to go on and do the GCE 'A' level, you would find this section useful even if you don't need it for the GCSE.

One of the most difficult concepts for students of accounting, and many owners of small businesses, to grasp is that the amount of profit recorded bears no relation at all to the amount of cash the firm actually has. Now that you have worked through this book, you should be able to see why.

- Sales figure includes credit sales, for which money has not yet been received.

- The valuation of stock may vary according to the method used (see Chapter 12).

- Amounts deducted from gross profit will include depreciation, and provision for bad debts. Both of these are estimated figures (see Chapters 6 and 7).

FORECASTING

There has to be some method of **forecasting** how much money in cash the business will need. This is absolutely vital, as virtually all businesses need to borrow money. The bank manager will want to see a realistic forecast of the business's prospects before he will lend the money. This is also useful in managing household expenses. Six months is usually the most feasible forecast period. You will need to draw up a chart such as the one shown in Fig. 42.

	JAN	FEB	MAR	APR	MAY	JUN
BALANCE AT START	300	400	500	600	700	800
+ RECEIPTS (FROM SALES)	1 000	1 000	1 000	1 000	1 000	1 000
	1 300	1 400	1 500	1 600	1 700	1 800
LESS EXPENSES	900	900	900	900	900	900
To C/fwd to next month	400	500	600	700	800	900

Fig. 42. Cash budget chart.

Suppose Jeremy Green sells about £1000 worth of goods every month. His outgoings are approximately £600 per month for purchases and £300 general expenses. In January he had £300 in cash. His cash budget may now be completed on these (estimated) figures. Although the figures are estimates, they can be fairly accurate if based on past records. His budget, beginning in January, will look like Figure 42.

You will see that Jeremy is going to be in a good position. As long as his sales and expenses remain the same he will have sufficient cash. If, however, his expenses or income had been variable, it would have been a useful way to discover whether Jeremy would need an overdraft or loan.

Try doing a cash flow budget for your own expenses.

Try this cash flow budget
Ivy Houseman owns a boutique. Her cash sales are approximately £2000 per month. She also runs a credit scheme and her sales on this are about £1500 per month. The debtors (on the credit scheme) always pay during the month following their purchases. Her expenses are approximately £350 a month, wages £500 each month. Draw up her cash budget for the next six months, beginning in January.

An exam question
Now do the question set out in Figure 43 from a 1989 exam paper, Northern Ireland Schools Examination Council (paper 3, question 3 part e).

SUMMARY
● Profit figures do not relate to cash.

- Cash budgets are designed to forecast future needs or sufficiency.

- Cash budgets make it possible to play the 'what if' game to help management decisions.

Fig. 43. Cash budget exam question.

(e) Below is Arnold's projected Cash Budget for the first six months of 1990.

RECEIPTS

	Jan	Feb	Mar	Apr	May	June	Total
Sales—Cash	1,000	1,000	1,500	1,500	1,500	1,500	8,000
Sales—Debtors	—	—	500	500	500	500	2,000
Capital	2,000						2,000
Total Receipts	3,000	1,000	2,000	2,000	2,000	2,000	12,000

PAYMENTS

	Jan	Feb	Mar	Apr	May	June	Total
Purchases—Cash	500	1,000	1,000	500	500	500	4,000
Purchases—Creditors	—	—	—	800	600	600	2,000
General Expenses	100	100	400	200	100	100	1,000
Fixtures and Fittings	490	1,500	510	—	—	—	2,500
Wages	300	300	300	300	400	400	2,000
Total Payments	1,390	2,900	2,210	1,800	1,600	1,600	11,500

CASH BUDGET

	Jan	Feb	Mar	Apr	May	June	Total
Opening Balance	—	1,610	(290)	(500)	(300)	100	—
Total Receipts	3,000	1,000	2,000	2,000	2,000	2,000	—
Total Payments	1,390	2,900	2,210	1,800	1,600	1,600	—
Closing Balances	1,610	(290)	(500)	(300)	100	500	—

(i) When is Arnold going to require financial assistance from his bank?

.... (2)

(ii) What would appear to be the principal reason for seeking financial assistance?

.... (2)

(iii) Why do you think there will be no income from Sales Debtors during January and February?

.... (3)

(iv) What change in purchasing pattern occurs from March–April onwards? Give *one* reason for your answer.

....

.... (3)

20
Taking the Exam

Everyone following the external syllabuses will have to take the exam, rather than be continually assessed on coursework.

To pass an exam, you must cultivate a positive attitude. You intend to pass with flying colours. Do not let anyone, especially yourself, make you think any differently! A faint heart gets faint results.

BEFORE THE EXAM

You will obviously need to revise. You have learned a lot of new and different techniques and procedures. You need to begin serious revision at least two months before the exam. If you don't have much time, concentrate on the things you found difficult.

The very best way to prepare for accounts exams is by doing lots of questions and answers. You will find the ones in this book useful, but will need more. Ask your teacher to set you some, or borrow other books from the library.

One of the problems with most text books is that they don't set out the answers. In GCSE it is the *method* which is all important. This is more important really than your arithmetic. You will be awarded marks for method, and for each correct part of an answer. This means you could still get nine out of ten, even if you have the wrong answer. That is why, in this book, all the answers are set out in full. Therefore you may have to ask your teacher to advise you on questions from other publications. Old exam papers are excellent, but, of course, you do need someone to give you the correct answers. The addresses of the examining boards are given on page 134. Past exam papers can be bought from them, usually quite cheaply. See the notes below on timing, and get used to doing the questions in the time allocated.

THE EXAM ITSELF

The main thing about accounts exams is that there is no time to waste. You must make the most of the time allocated. You must spread yourself equally throughout the questions. You can only achieve full marks for each question, no more. It is no use answering one or two questions absolutely wonderfully, but neglecting others. You *must* obtain marks for *each* question.

In the GCSE exam, the examiners do tell you how many marks are allocated to each question. It is the small figure, usually in brackets, given after each question, or part of a question. This is your guide. Suppose there were 120 marks in the whole paper, and the paper was to last two hours. That would mean that you could afford to spend one minute for each mark, so if a question was given as being worth 25 marks, you would know that you could spend 25 minutes on it. In fact, you will probably find that you can do most of the questions quicker than this. Just divide the total number of marks by the number of minutes allowed for the exam.

If you are finding a question somewhat difficult, leave it for the time being. You can come back to it when you have safely completed all the questions you find easier. You may usually do the questions in any order, as long as you remember to *indicate clearly* which question you are answering. It may give you more confidence to tackle the easier questions first. At least you will know that you have gained some valuable marks already.

Friends will wish you luck, but remember that passing an exam has more to do with preparation and technique (as above) than luck.

SUMMARY

• Practise as many questions as you can, especially in your weakest areas.

• Make sure you set out, and label, your answers correctly.

• Watch the time. Pace yourself so that you give equal time to all questions.

• Be positive. You know you can't fail if you've prepared properly.

21
Answers to Exercises

These answers are designed to be a learning method. That is why they are all fully set out where applicable. If you find them difficult, do not despair. Just keep studying the answers and trying to do them again yourself.

In some cases, notes have been added to help you. Don't forget, the more times you do these exercises, the more you are learning. Practise is the very best way to succeed in accounting. Some of the double entry exercises seem very involved. These would actually be easier in a real-life situation.

Don't forget that double entry is only one small section of the whole syllabus. Many students feel very 'bogged down' by this section. Don't let it put you off. It is probably the most tedious section, until you have mastered it. Then it becomes very simple and straightforward.

As stated in the acknowledgements, the examining boards are in no way responsible for the answers to exam questions. In some cases there may be more than one way to tackle a question. The answers given here are generally the easiest way.

CHAPTER 1

GEMMA JACKSON   CASH BOOK

DATE	DETAILS	CASH	BANK	DATE	DETAILS	CASH	BANK
	BAL B/d	25	30				
JUN 1	CASH SALES	30		JUN 2	RENT		40
				5	GOODS	10	
11	CHEQUE RECEIVED		75	9	PHONE		50
				17	WINDOW CLEANER	5	

Fig. 44. Answer for Chapter 1, page 12.

GEMMA JACKSON   CASH BOOK

DATE	DETAILS	CASH	BANK	DATE	DETAILS	CASH	BANK
JUNE 1	BAL B/d	5	30	JUN 6	RENT		35
3	CHEQUE RECEIVED		10	10	WAGES	20	
5	CASH SALES	25		12	PAID OUT		40
6	CASH SALES	10					
12	CASH SALES	20					
	To c/d		35		To c/d	40	
		60	75			60	75
	BAL b/d	40			BAL B/d		35

Fig. 45. Answer for Chapter 1, page 14.

DATE	DETAILS	DISCOUNT	CASH	BANK
JULY 1	BALANCES B/d		40	
2	CHEQUE RECEIVED	2		38
4	CASH SALES PAID INTO BANK			30
20	CASH SALES		10	
		2	50	68
	BALANCES B/d		30	9.25

DATE	DETAILS	DISCOUNT	CASH	BANK
JULY 1	BALANCE B/d			35
15	PAID SUPPLIER	1.25		23.75
25	PAID CLEANER		20	
	BALANCES To C/d		30	9.25
		1.25	50	68.00

Fig. 46. Answer for Chapter 1, page 15.

CASH BOOK OF MOVANE ENTERPRISES

A / B

DATE	DETAILS	DISCOUNT	CASH	BANK
MAR 1	BALANCE B/d		50	
2	SALES			2400
4	W. SCOTT	5		540
4	BANK (CONTRA)		400	
		5	90	2940
MAR 6	BALANCES B/d		62	310

DATE	DETAILS	DISCOUNT	CASH	BANK
MAR 1	BALANCE B/d			1150
3	CLEANERS		28	
3	P. MURPHY			1000
4	CASH (CONTRA)			400
5	SALARIES			440
5	BALANCE c/d			310
			90	2940

C. CASH IN HAND NOW 62. FIRM NOW HAS 310 IN ITS BANK ACCOUNT – NO LONGER ANY OVERDRAFT

D. TO ENCOURAGE PROMPT PAYMENT OF INVOICES

E. TRANSFER OF FUNDS FROM CASH TO BANK OR VICE-VERSA.

Fig. 47. Answer for Chapter 1, page 16.

CHAPTER 2

John Moss

CASH Book

DATE	DETAILS	CASH	BANK	DATE	DETAILS	CASH	BANK
	BAL B/d	50	500				
					PURCHASES		350
	SALES	515			RENT	20	
					EQUIPMENT		150
					PETROL	50	
					c/d	495	
		565	500			565	500
	Bal B/d	495					

AS THE BANK COLUMNS ARE THE SAME THERE IS NOTHING TO c/d THERE.

PURCHASES

DATE	DETAILS	DR	CR	BAL
	BAL B/d			250
	PRODUCE	350		500

SALES

DATE	DETAILS	DR	CR	BAL
	BAL B/d			320 cr
	CASH		515	835 cr

RENT

DATE	DETAILS	DR	CR	BAL
	BAL B/d			20
	CASH	20		40

EQUIPMENT

DATE	DETAILS	DR	CR	BAL
	SCALES (BANK)	150		150

PETROL

DATE	DETAILS	DR	CR	BAL
	CASH	50		50

Fig. 48. Answer for Chapter 2, page 21.

MANDY BAXTER

CASH BOOK

DATE	DETAILS	CASH	BANK	DATE	DETAILS	CASH	BANK
	CAPITAL		5500		EQUIPMENT		60
	BANK	100c			CASH		100c
	CASH SALES	2350			FIXTURES		1500
	CASH		2350c		RENT		1200
					BANK	2350c	
					VIAGO		2450
					BAL c/d	100	2540
		2450	7850			2450	7850
	BAL B/d	100	2540				

CAPITAL

DATE	DETAILS	DR	CR	BAL
	BANK		5500	5500 cr

EQUIPMENT

DATE	DETAILS	DR	CR	BAL
	TILL (BANK)	60		60

FIXTURES

DATE	DETAILS	DR	CR	BAL
	BANK	1500		1500

VIAGO CLOTHING

DATE	DETAILS	DR	CR	BAL
	STOCK OF CLOTHES		2450	2450 cr

PURCHASES

DATE	DETAILS	DR	CR	BAL
	VIAGO	2450		2450

SALES

DATE	DETAILS	DR	CR	BAL
	CASH		2350	2350 cr

RENT

DATE	DETAILS	DR	CR	BAL
	BANK	1200		1200

Fig. 49. Answer for Chapter 2, page 26.

Notes on Mandy Baxter

Note that when she paid Virgo Clothing the entry was:

- credit, cash book
- debit, Virgo Clothing.

This brings the account to nil.

The purchase on credit was still entered in the purchases account. The Virgo account replaced the cash book entry temporarily. Then when she paid Virgo, the amount was cleared from their account and was entered in the cash book.

All sales and purchases (for re-sale) are entered in the sales and purchases accounts respectively, whether they are paid for immediately or not.

If you had entered the till in the fixtures and fittings account, rather than equipment, this would be acceptable. Different firms have their own ways, and names, for accounts.

HARRY WEBSTER

CASH BOOK

DATE	DETAILS	CASH	BANK	DATE	DETAILS	CASH	BANK
OCT1	CAPITAL		5000	OCT2	MACHINERY		2650
OCT4	SALES	23		OCT8	ALPHA		100
OCT8	SALES	50					
					BAL c/d	73	2250
		73	5000			73	5000
	BAL B/d	73	2250				

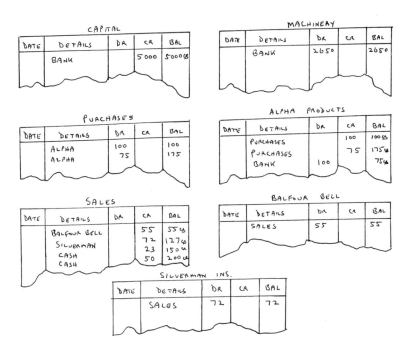

CAPITAL

DATE	DETAILS	DR	CR	BAL
	BANK		5000	5000 CR

MACHINERY

DATE	DETAILS	DR	CR	BAL
	BANK	2650		2650

PURCHASES

DATE	DETAILS	DR	CR	BAL
	ALPHA	100		100
	ALPHA	75		175

ALPHA PRODUCTS

DATE	DETAILS	DR	CR	BAL
	PURCHASES		100	100 CR
	PURCHASES		75	175 CR
	BANK	100		75 CR

SALES

DATE	DETAILS	DR	CR	BAL
	BALFOUR BELL		55	55 CR
	SILVERMAN		72	127 CR
	CASH		23	150 CR
	CASH		50	200 CR

BALFOUR BELL

DATE	DETAILS	DR	CR	BAL
	SALES	55		55

SILVERMAN INS.

DATE	DETAILS	DR	CR	BAL
	SALES	72		72

Fig. 50. Answer for Chapter 2, page 26.

MARY MARTIN

CASH BOOK

DATE	DETAILS	CASH	BANK	DATE	DETAILS	CASH	BANK
	CAPITAL		6200		TOUCHWOOD ENTERPRISES		2300
	CASH SALE	73.56			RENT		100
					WINDOW CLEANER	5	
					DRAWINGS	25	
					BAL c/d	43.56	3800
		73.56	6200			73.56	6200
	BAL B/d	43.56	3800				

CAPITAL (NOMINAL LEDGER)

DATE	DETAILS	DR	CR	BAL
	BANK		6200	6200 B

EQUIPMENT (NOMINAL LEDGER)

DATE	DETAILS	DR	CR	BAL
	BANK	2300		2300

SALES DAY BOOK

DATE	DETAILS	INVOICE AMOUNT	VAT	TOTAL
	A. SOUTH	50	8.75	58.75
	A. SOUTH	45	7.88	52.88
	M. SUGDEN	50	8.75	58.75
		145	25.38	

SALES RETURNS DAY BOOK

DETAILS	CR NOTE AMOUNT	VAT	TOTAL
M. SUGDEN	12.50	2.19	14.69

PURCHASES DAY BOOK

DATE	DETAILS	INVOICE AMOUNT	VAT	TOTAL
	PAPER PATH	200	35	235
	PAPER PATH	75	13.13	88.13
		275	48.13	

PURCHASE RETURNS DAY BOOK

DETAILS	CR. NOTE AMOUNT	VAT	TOTAL
PAPER PATH	25	4.38	29.38

Fig. 51. Answer for Chapter 2, page 30.

MARY MARTIN (continued)

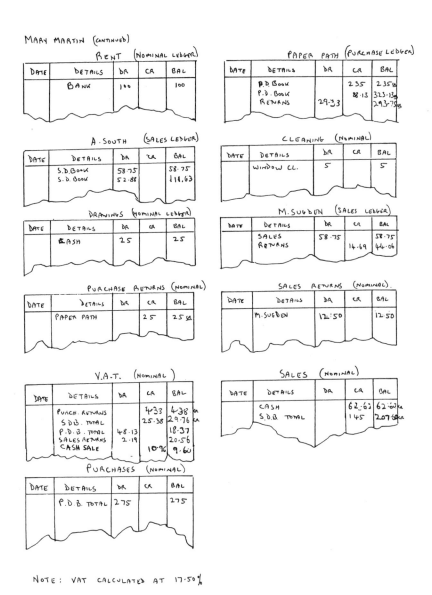

RENT (NOMINAL LEDGER)

DATE	DETAILS	DR	CR	BAL
	BANK	100		100

A. SOUTH (SALES LEDGER)

DATE	DETAILS	DR	CR	BAL
	S.D. Book	58.75		58.75
	S.D. Book	52.88		111.63

DRAWINGS (NOMINAL LEDGER)

DATE	DETAILS	DR	CR	BAL
	CASH	25		25

PURCHASE RETURNS (NOMINAL)

DATE	DETAILS	DR	CR	BAL
	PAPER PATH		25	25 ca

V.A.T. (NOMINAL)

DATE	DETAILS	DR	CR	BAL
	PURCH. RETURNS		4.38	4.38 ca
	S.D.B. TOTAL		25.38	29.76 ca
	P.D.B. TOTAL	48.13		18.37
	SALES RETURNS	2.19		20.56
	CASH SALE		10.96	9.60

PURCHASES (NOMINAL)

DATE	DETAILS	DR	CR	BAL
	P.D.B. TOTAL	275		275

PAPER PATH (PURCHASE LEDGER)

DATE	DETAILS	DR	CR	BAL
	P.D. Book		235	235 cr
	P.D. Book		88.13	323.13 cr
	RETURNS	29.33		293.79 cr

CLEANING (NOMINAL)

DATE	DETAILS	DR	CR	BAL
	WINDOW CL.	5		5

M. SUGDEN (SALES LEDGER)

DATE	DETAILS	DR	CR	BAL
	SALES	58.75		58.75
	RETURNS		14.69	44.06

SALES RETURNS (NOMINAL).

DATE	DETAILS	DR	CR	BAL
	M. SUGDEN	12.50		12.50

SALES (NOMINAL)

DATE	DETAILS	DR	CR	BAL
	CASH		62.60	62.60 cr
	S.D.B. TOTAL		145	207.60 cr

NOTE: VAT CALCULATED AT 17.50%

Fig. 52. Answer for Chapter 2, page 30.

J. GLENDENNING

J. HARYOTT

DATE	DETAILS	DR.	CR.	BAL.
AUG 1	BALANCE			500 <u>a</u>
4	PURCHASES		1400	1900
10	RETURNS	96		1804
14	CHEQUE	450		1354
	DISCOUNT	50		1304
28	ERROR ON DISCOUNT		25	1329
SEP 1	BALANCE			1329

K. FELLOWES

DATE	DETAILS	DR.	CR.	BAL.
AUG 1	BALANCE			670 <u>cr</u>
5	PURCHASES		890	1560
19	CREDIT NOTE	40		1520
SEP 1	BALANCE			1520

NOTE: IN PRACTICE YOU MAY NOT HAVE TO RULE OFF AND RE-WRITE THE BALANCES. HOWEVER, IF AN EXAM QUESTION SPECIFICALLY REQUESTS BALANCE AT A CERTAIN DATE, THIS IS THE 'SAFEST' WAY TO DO IT.

Fig. 53. Answer for Chapter 2, page 31.

CHAPTER 3

Harry Webster's total balance totals 5275.

Spotting errors in the trial balance
1. Commission
2. Original entry
3. Omission
4. Reversal of entries
5. Principle
6. Compensating

Exam question
1. A trial balance is a list of balances taken from the accounts in a double entry book-keeping system.

2. The purpose is to test the arithmetical accuracy of the book-keeping.

3.

4. Any four of the six listed above, 1-6.

5. None of them would upset the balance between debits and credits. Refer to the chapter and give a detailed explanation of two of them.

6. Use any four examples from the first question of this chapter, which asked you to name the type of error.

7. a. Equal value: this could mean that one half of a double entry has been missed off, or something may be included in the records which shouldn't be there.
b. Half the difference: This would mean that an item could have been debited instead of credited, or vice versa. For this reason it would also be advisable to look for items of twice the value.

CHAPTER 4
B.Burton's account
B.Burton trading and profit and loss account for y/e . . .

Sales		10000
Opening stock	2950	
Purchases	4850	
	7800	
Closing stock	3270	
Cost of sales		4530
Gross profit		5470
Expenses		
Travelling expenses	420	
Administration expenses	310	
Electricity	500	
		1230
Net profit		4240

N.Iveson's account
N.Iveson trading and profit and loss account for y/e . . .

Sales		15000
Opening stock	4500	
Purchases	21000	
	25500	
Closing stock	3200	
		22300
Gross loss		(7300)
Expenses		500
Net loss		(7800)

You will see that the result is not always a profit! Note that accountants put figures in **brackets** to denote a **minus figure**.

N.Carter's account
Nathan Carter trading and profit and loss account for the year ended . . .

Sales			25713
Less returns inward			235
			25478
Opening stock		10000	
Purchases	19642		
Add carriage inwards	242		
	19884		
Less returns outward	150		
		19734	
		29734	
Less closing stock		14000	
			15734
Gross profit			9744
Expenses			
Salaries	4214		
Admin. expenses	2231		
Rent	3210		
			9655
Net profit			89

An exam question

J.Baker trading and profit and loss account for the quarter ended 31 Dec 1988.

Sales			37000
Less returns inwards			250
			36750
Opening stock		5000	
Purchases	25000		
Add carriage inward	750		
	25750		
Less returns outward	900		
		24850	
		29850	
Closing stock		4500	
Cost of sales			25350
			11400
Wages (trading account)			9500
Gross profit			1900
Expenses			
Carriage outwards	1050		
Selling expenses	750		
			1800
Net profit			100

Profit adjustments

a. −

b. +

c. −

d. + because you would enter the profit and loss account from the rent account.

An exam question

2. −620
3. + 680
4. + 10000 (adjust purchases!)
5. −300
6. + 400

N.Barlow's account

Trading and profit and loss account for N.Barlow for the year ended . . . (date)

Sales		23000
Opening stock	7500	
Purchases	15000	
	22500	
Closing stock	5500	
Cost of sales		17000
Gross profit		6000
Insurance	800	
Less in advance	200	
	600	
Electricity	650	
Less last year's	150	
	500	
Administration	2300	
Wages/salaries	16000	
		19400
Net loss		(13400)

Note that both prepayment and accrual are deducted, as neither of them belongs to this year.

If owing for *this* year it would be added on.

CHAPTER 5

Draw up a balance sheet

B.Bertram balance sheet as at . . .

Fixed assets			
Premises			28000
Van			5000
			33000
Current assets			
Stock	4000		
Debtors	2500		
Bank	1000		
	7500		
Current liabilities			
Creditors		3000	
Working capital			4500
Net worth			37500
Financed by:			
Capital	30000		
+ net profit	8000		
		38000	
Less drawings		500	
		37500	

G.Cooper profit and loss account for the year ended . . .

Sales			40000
Purchases	30000		
Closing stock	10000		
Cost of sales			20000
Gross profit			20000
Expenses			
Insurance	500		
Wages	5000		
Rates	3000		
Electricity	2000		
		10500	
Net profit		9500	

G.Cooper balance sheet as at . . .

Fixed assets			
Premises		30000	
Fittings		5000	
Van		6500	
		41500	
Current Assets			
Stock	10000		
Debtors	7000		
Bank	10000		
		27000	
Current liabilities			
Creditors		4000	
Working capital		23000	
Net worth		64500	
Financed by:			
Capital	59000		
+ net profit	9500		
		68500	
Less drawings		4000	
		64500	

Exercises in balance sheets
Jason Green balance sheet as at 31 May 1989

Fixed assets

Premises		60000
Fixtures and fittings		12000
		72000

Current assets

Stock	15000		
Debtors	4000		
Cash	200		
Prepaid expenses	800		
		20000	

Current liabilities

Expense creditors	580		
Trade creditors	2000		
Bank overdraft	1420		
		4000	
Working capital			16000
			88000

Long term liabilities

Mortgage on premises		6000
Net worth		82000

Financed by Capital		89000
Less drawings	6000	
Net loss	1000	
		7000
		82000

Note that the amount prepaid by Jason is a current asset.

The bank overdraft is a current liability. The definition of a current liability is anything falling due within one year. A bank overdraft can be called in any time, and so is classed as a current liability. ·

CHAPTER 6

I. 1450. 2. 1500, 1275, 1084. 3. 35.

Z , G CASTINGS

PROVISION FOR DEPRECIATION

DATE	DETAILS	DR	CR	BAL
YR 1			600	600
YR 2			480	1080
YR 3			384	1464

BALANCE SHEET EXTRACTS.		COST	ACC. DEP.	NET.
YR 1.	MACHINE	3000	600	2400
YR 2.	MACHINE	3000	1080	1920
YR 3.	MACHINE	3000	1464	1536

A . B . ENGINEERING

BALANCE SHEET EXTRACTS

		COST	ACC. DEP	NET
YR. 1.	MACHINE	20,000	2000	18000
YR. 2	MACHINE	20,000	4000	16000
YR. 3.	MACHINE	20000	6000	14000

IN PROFIT + LOSS A/C

1st YR	2000
2nd YR	2000
3rd YR	2000

Fig. 54. Answer for Chapter 6, page 60.

CHAPTER 7

The amounts in Figures 55, 56 and 57 are rounded to the nearest pound.

B. TAGGART

BAD   DEBTS

DATE	DETAILS	DR	CR	BAL
	WRITTEN OFF A/cs	750		750

PROVISION FOR BAD DEBTS

DATE	DETAILS	DR	CR	BAL
	(7% OF 5000)		350	350

PROFIT + LOSS ACCOUNT

DR   750
DR   350

(DR IN PROFIT + LOSS MEANS IT WILL BE DEDUCTED).

BALANCE SHEET ENTRY

CURRENT ASSETS

   DEBTORS   5000

   LESS PROVISION FOR   350

   BAD DEBTS   4650

Fig. 55. Answer for Chapter 7, page 64.

M. BEDWIN

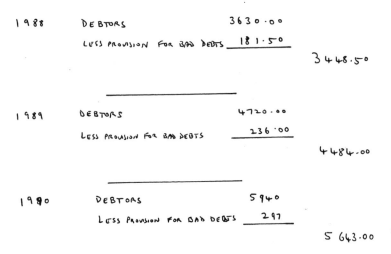

PROVISION FOR BAD DEBTS

DATE	DETAILS	DR	CR	BAL
1988			181·50	181·50
1989			54·50	236·00
1990			61·00	297·00

PROFIT + LOSS A/c

1988	DR	181·50
1989	DR	54·50
1990	DR	61·00

BALANCE SHEET EXTRACTS

1988	DEBTORS	3630·00
	LESS PROVISION FOR BAD DEBTS	181·50
		3448·50

1989	DEBTORS	4720·00
	LESS PROVISION FOR BAD DEBTS	236·00
		4484·00

1980	DEBTORS	5940
	LESS PROVISION FOR BAD DEBTS	297
		5643·00

Fig. 56. Answer for Chapter 7, page 65.

M. COX.

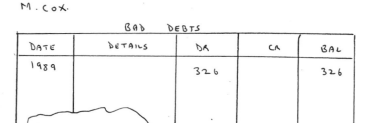

BAD DEBTS

DATE	DETAILS	DR	CR	BAL
1989		326		326

PROVISION FOR BAD DEBTS

DATE	DETAILS	DR	CR	BAL
1989			491	491
1990			71	562

PROFIT + LOSS A/c ENTRIES

1989	DR	491
1989	DR	326
1990	DR	71

BALANCE SHEET EXTRACT

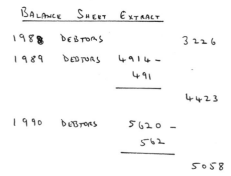

1988	DEBTORS		3226
1989	DEBTORS	4914 –	
		491	
		———	
			4423
1990	DEBTORS	5620 –	
		562	
		———	
			5058

Fig. 57. Answer for Chapter 7, page 65.

CHAPTER 8

Working out the types of cost
prime
prime
prime
production
production
production
prime
production
production
production

A manufacturing account

Stock of raw materials at start	650	
+ purchases	1000	
		1650
Less raw materials at end	700	
		950
Cost of raw materials consumed		
Direct wages	3000	
Royalties	300	
		3300
Prime cost		4250
Factory overheads		
Rent	900	
Depreciation	400	
Maintenance wages	2000	
Parts for repairs	100	
		3400
Production cost of completed goods		7650

B. Best's account

Manufacturing and trading and profit and loss accounts for B. Best for the year ended . . .

Stock of raw materials at start		3000
Purchases	9000	
+ carriage	500	
	——	9500
		12500
Stock of raw materials at end		4000
		——
Cost of raw materials consumed		8500
Direct wages		7000
		——
Prime cost		15500
Factory expenses	3000	
Canteen expenses	1000	
	——	
		4000
		——
Production cost of finished goods		19500
		——
Sales		40000
Opening stock finished goods	5000	
Production cost finished goods	19500	
	——	
	24500	
Closing stock of finished goods	3500	
	——	
Cost of sales		21000
		——
Gross profit		19000
Administration expenses	6000	
Selling and distribution expenses	7500	
Depreciation of office equipment	500	
Provision for bad debts	350	
	——	
		14350
		——
Net profit		4650
		——

CHAPTER 9

Preparing a receipts and payments account

Income and expenditure account for the Wolds Way Rambling Club for the year ended . . .

Working
―――――

Trading account for refreshments		
Sales of refreshments		15
Refreshments at start	12	
Purchases	7	
	19	
Refreshments at end	10	
		9
Gross profit on refreshments		6

Income		
Subs received		250
Profit on refreshments		6
Rucksacks—sold	350	
—bought	200	
Profit on rucksacks		150
Income form coffee morning		65
Total income		471
Expenditure		
Fees for speaker		25
Rent for village halls		35
Total expenditure		60
Surplus of income over expenditure		411

An exam question

**Radcliffe Social Club. Receipts and payments account for
year ended 31 December 1988**

Receipts		Payments	
890 b/d			
3200			670
46000			2500
			860
			38500
		balance	7560
	_____		_____
50090			50090
	_____		_____

7560 b/d

**Income and expenditure account for the year ended 31
December 1988**

Income		
Subs 3200-150 next year's	3050	
Admissions	46000	
	_____	
		49050
Expenditure		
Rates	670	
Lighting and heating 860 + 90 owing	950	
Fees paid	38500	
	_____	
		40120
		_____
Surplus of income over expenditure		8930
		_____

Note: although £5000 was incurred during the period, £2500 of
this is classed as a short-term loan, and will therefore appear in
the balance sheet as a current liability rather than be deducted as
expenditure. The notes said that it was repayable within one year,
so it will be in *next* year's account.

Balance sheet as at 31 December 1988

Fixed assets		
Furniture		5000
Current assets		
Bank	7560	
Current liabilities		
Subs in advance	150	
Short term loan (furniture)	2500	
Electricity bill owing	90	
	2740	
		4820
Net assets (net worth)		9820
Financed by		
Cash at start	890	
+ surplus	8930	
		9820

CHAPTER 10

Appropriation account exercise

Partnership appropriation account of Green, Cross and Bowles

Net profit		35000
Interest on drawings: Green	600	
Cross	400	
Bowles	400	
	———	
		1400
		———
		36400
Salary for Green		12000
		———
		24400
Interest on capital: Green	400	
Cross	500	
Bowles	500	
	———	
		1400
		———
		23000
Share of profit: Green	4600	
Cross	9200	
Bowles	9200	
	———	
		23000
		———

1. An exam question
- Drawings are money taken out of the business by the owner(s) for his/their own use.

- Interest on drawings is money charged to the owner(s) on the drawings taken out. It discourages the taking of too much in drawings.

- Provision for depreciation is an amount calculated to set against the value of assets. The purpose is to avoid overstating the profits or worth of the business.

- Working capital is calculated by deducting current liabilities from current assets. It is the liquid asset amount which is in constant flux within the business.

- Interest on capital is the amount the business pays to the owner(s) on the amount of capital he/they have put in to the business.

2. i **Bunker and Lake profit and loss appropriation account for the year ended 31 December 1988**

Net trading profit		40600
Interest on drawings:		
Bunker	400	
Lake	1800	
		2200
		42800
Interest on capital:		
Bunker (40000 x 8 per cent)	3200	
Lake (50000 x 8 per cent)	4000	
		7200
		35600
Share of profits:		
Bunker	17800	
Lake	17800	
	35600	

CURRENT ACCOUNTS

BUNKER

DETAILS	DR	CR	BAL
BALANCE			8400 cr
DRAWINGS	24000		15600
INTEREST ON DRAWINGS	400		16000
INTEREST ON CAPITAL		3200	12800
SHARE OF PROFIT		17800	5000 cr

LAKE

DETAILS	DR	CR	BAL
BALANCE			4120
DRAWINGS	30000		34120
INTEREST ON DRAWINGS	1800		35920
INTEREST ON CAPITAL		4000	31920
SHARE OF PROFIT		17800	14120

Fig. 58. Answer for Chapter 10, page 80, question 2aii.

b.Balance sheet for Bunker and Lake as at 31 December 1988

Fixed assets

	cost	dep	net
Premises			100000
Motor van	12000	9000	3000
			103000

Current assets

Debtors	6420		
Cash at bank	6596		
		13016	

Current liabilities

Wages accrued	3936		
Interest owing	1200		
		5136	

Working capital			7880
Net assets			110880
Less long term loan			30000
Net worth			80880

Financed by
Partners' capital accounts:

Bunker	40000	
Lake	50000	
		90000

Add credit current account

Bunker		5000
		95000

Less debit current account

Lake		14120
		80880

Note: Current accounts, like the capital account, are usually credit balances. They represent what the business owes to the partner.

In this case, Lake has a debit balance. This represents what *he* owes to the business.

CHAPTER 11

N.Rose & Co
Required for distribution:
75000 x 8% preference shares = 6000
100000 x 12% ordinary shares + 12000

18000

An exam question

a. **Streamline plc profit and loss appropriation account for the year ended 31 December 1990**

Profit and loss balance b/fwd		34000
Net profit for year		15000
		49000
Transfer to general reserve		20000
		29000
Preference share dividend	1000	
Ordinary share dividend	18000	
		19000
Unappropriated profit		10000

b. **Balance sheet as at 31 December 1990**

Fixed assets cost dep net

	cost	dep	net
Premises	250000		250000
Plant and machinery	140000	50000	90000
			340000

Current assets			
Stock	16540		
Debtors	12080		
Bank	15280		
Prepaid advertising	2000		
		45900	

Current liabilities			
Creditors	3000		
Wages owing	3900		
Proposed dividend	19000		
		25900	

Working capital			20000
Net worth			360000

Financed by:			
Authorised share capital			520000

Issued share capital:			
Ordinary shares		300000	
Preference shares		20000	
			320000
General reserve + new		30000	
Unappropriated profit		10000	
			40000
			360000

CHAPTER 12

An exam question
a. Criticism in this instance means appraisal of contents.
Forge Engineering:

- has a more valuable premises (by 20000);

- has more machinery (by 10000);

- has more money owing to it by debtors (by 6200);

- has stock which is depreciating;

- has a greater amount of share capital;

- has almost twice as much undistributed profits as Metal Products;

- has a large bank overdraft (whereas Metal Products has a bank balance of £200);

- owes £6000 more to its creditors than Metal Products does.

b. Previous year's balance sheet and profit and loss account for both years would be useful, then it would be possible to also do a flow of funds.

c. Accounting ratios: eg current ratio, acid test ratio, working capital. You are limited owing to the lack of information available.

d. The Metal Products Ltd is in a good position of liquidity and could be safely taken over, although it would be desirable to have the necessary figures to calculate the profitability ratio:

$$\frac{\text{net profit}}{\text{sales x 100}} = \text{per centage profitability}$$

The other firm, Forge Engineering, is not such a good proposition. Not only is it in a poor state of liquidity, but also has a large bank overdraft.

Note: It is purely a matter of opinion which firm (if either) to take over. This is one of those questions with no right or wrong answer. It is just a matter of bringing out your knowledge in your answer.

CHAPTER 13

Practice sheet for flow of funds statement (1)
KS Alarms
Sources of funds

Increase in creditors	6800	
Net profit	9700	
Loan	4000	
		20500

Application of funds

Increase in fixed assets	20000	
Increase in stock	5000	
Increase in debtors	2500	
		27500
Excess of application over sources		(7000)

Proof:

Cash at start	12000
Cash at end	5000
Cash used	7000

Practice sheet for flow of funds statement (2)
J.Bird
Sources of funds

Increase in creditors	700	
Net profit	14500	
		15200

Application of funds

Inc in fixed assets	10000	
Inc in stock	1650	
Inc in debtors	2300	
Drawings	4750	
		18700
Excess of application over sources		(3500)

Proof:

Bank at start	2000	
Bank at end o/d	(1500)	
Cash used		3500

CHAPTER 14

Alfred Smith's business
Trading and profit and loss account as at . . .

Sales = total of invoices sent =		744
+ cash received		53
		797
Opening stock	490	
Purchases	352	
	842	
Closing stock	350	
Cost of sales		492
Gross profit		305
Expenses		178
Net profit		
		127

Balance sheet as at . . .

Current assets		
Stock	350	
Debtors	744	
Bank	976	
Net assets	2070	
Financed by:		
Capital at start	?	
+ net profit	127	
	2070	

Here you have to deduce that the capital at start was £1943. Note that balance sheets do not always look quite as you might expect!

CHAPTER 15

Will Grant's account

Sales			3300
Opening stock	3200		
Purchases	2600		
	———		
		5800	
Closing stock		3600	
		———	
Cost of sales			2200
			———
Gross profit			1100
			———

It is easier to work the whole thing out if you do a trading account as above. Just leave blanks for now where the figures are unknown. You can fill them in as you go.

First find the closing stock: 3400 x 2 - 3200 = 3600.

Now you will be able to do the cost of sales.

Now if mark up is 50 per cent then the profit must be 50 per cent of cost—so it's 50 per cent of 2200 = 1100.

You know that if mark up is 50 per cent then margin will be 33 1/3 per cent so profit must be 1/3 of sales.

So sales are 3 x profit = 3300.

An exam question

Stock value at 4 June	7600
Less purchases	840
	———
	6760
Add sales (see workings)	880
	———
	7640
Less return	48
	———
	7592
Add drawn	30
	———
Corrected net profit	7622
	———

Workings:

Takings at tills	820
Add credit sales	280
	————
	1100

Mark up = 25 per cent (1/4) so margin on sales is 20 per cent (1/5)
1100 less 20 per cent = 880
60 less 20 per cent = 48

CHAPTER 16

Exercise in reconciling
Corrected cash book balance

Balance	315
Add standing order	37
	————
	352
Less charges	10
	————
Corrected cash book balance	342
	————

Bank reconciliation

Bank statement balance	114
Add cheques not credited:	
K.Petty	106
C.Ashton	92
G.Robin	62
	————
	374
Less cheque paid out	32
	————
Real balance	342
	————

An exam question

1. Any three of the following:
   Credit transfer (26.89)
   Standing order (93.56)
   Bank charges (18.50)
   Unpresented cheque (12.67)
   Cheque not credited (210.50)

2. Cheques are not presented to the bank for payment in the same order that you enter them.

3.

BANK ACCOUNT

BAL. B/d	524.27	STANDING ORDER	93.56
CREDIT TRANSFER	26.89	BANK CHARGES	18.50
		BAL TO c/d	439.10
	551.56		551.56
BAL B/d	439.10		

Fig. 59. Answer for Chapter 16, page 111.

Bank reconciliation statement

Balance as bank statement	241.27
Add cheques not credited	210.50
	451.77
Less cheques not presented	12.67
Balance	439.10

Last question: Four of the same reasons as in part 1 above.

CHAPTER 17

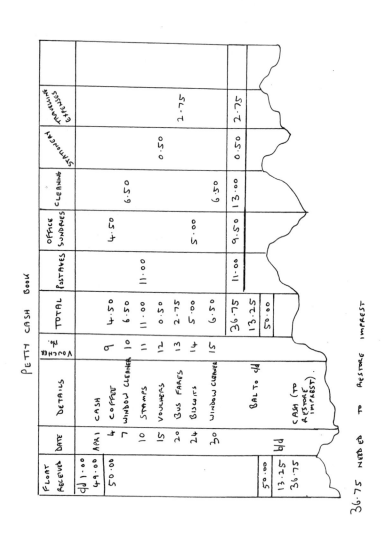

PETTY CASH BOOK

Float Received	Date	Details	Voucher No.	Total	Postages	Office Sundries	Cleaning	Stationery	Travelling Expenses
c/d 1.00 / 49.00 / 50.00	APR 1	CASH							
	4	COFFEE	9	4.50		4.50			
	7	WINDOW CLEANER	10	6.50			6.50		
	10	STAMPS	11	11.00	11.00				
	15	VOUCHERS	12	0.50				0.50	
	20	BUS FARES	13	2.75					2.75
	24	BISCUITS	14	5.00		5.00			
	30	WINDOW CLEANER	15	6.50			6.50		
		BAL TO c/d		36.75	11.00	9.50	13.00	0.50	2.75
50.00				13.25					
13.25	b/d	CASH (TO RESTORE IMPREST)		50.00					
36.75									

36.75 NEEDED TO RESTORE IMPREST

Fig. 60. Answer for Chapter 17, page 116.

An exam question

a. Brian has petty cash vouchers with the signatures of the people to whom he has given money.

Receipts	Date	Details	Voucher Number	Total Payments	Cleaning	Postage	Travelling Expenses
			PETTY CASH BOOK				
25.00	Sep 8	BALANCE					
	8	BUS FARES	85	0.60			0.60
	8	POSTAGE	86	3.40		3.40	
	9	W. CLEANER	87	4.00	4.00		
	10	TAXI	88	3.00			3.00
	10	RAIL FARE	89	10.00			10.00
	12	STAMPS	90	2.10		2.10	
				23.10	4.00	5.50	13.60
		BAL TO c/d →		1.90			
25 00				25.00			
1 90		←BAL b/d					
23 10		BAL GIVEN TO RESTORE IMPREST					

Fig. 61. Answer for Chapter 17, page 117.

CHAPTER 18

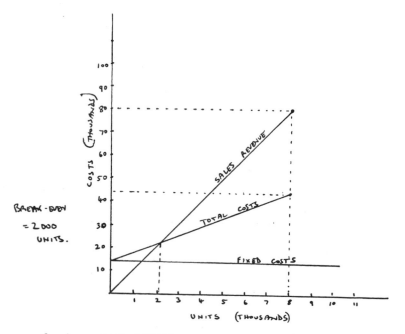

JASON ROSE.
BREAK EVEN CHART.

To PLOT SALES REVENUE :-

    EXP. SALES × REV = 8000 × (PRICE PER UNIT) £10 = 80,000
PLOT FROM 8000 (EXP. SALES) TO 80,000 COSTS AND DRAW
LINE FROM 0 TO THIS POINT.

To PLOT TOTAL COSTS :-

    (VAR. COSTS × EXP. SALES) + FIXED COSTS = (£4 × 8000) + 12000 = 44000
PLOT FROM EXP SALES (8000 UNITS) TO 44000. DRAW LINE
FROM FIXED COSTS TO THIS POINT.

Fig. 62.

An exam question

a.

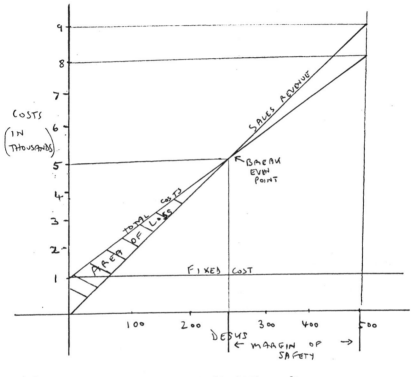

BREAK EVEN GRAPH

FIXED COSTS = 1000   TOTAL COSTS = 9000
SALES REVENUE = 1000   MARGIN = $\frac{1}{4}$ PER DESK
SALES REVENUE AT BREAK EVEN = 5000.

Fig. 63. Answer for Chapter 18, page 122.

b. 250 desks.

c. Break even point will remain constant, but the area of profit will be larger.

Note: you could draw a rough version of your graph to prove this to yourself. However, if you have understood the principles, this answer should be obvious to you.

d. Formula = fixed costs   =   1000

$$\frac{}{\text{selling price—variable cost}} \quad \frac{}{20-16}$$

Now = 1000

$$\frac{1000}{20-18 \ (16+12.50\%)}$$

= 1000

$$\frac{1000}{2}$$

Answer = 500 units
Sales revenue at break even = 500 x £20 = £10000

CHAPTER 19

CASH BUDGET FOR IVY HOUSEMAN

	JAN	FEB	MAR	APR	MAY	JUN
BALANCE AT START	–	1150	3800	6450	9100	11750
RECEIPTS	2000	3500	3500	3500	3500	3500
	2000	4650	7300	9950	12600	15250
EXPENSES	850	850	850	850	850	850
BALANCE AT END	1150	3800	6450	9100	11750	14400

Fig. 64. Answer for Chapter 19, page 124.

An exam question
i. Arnold will need financial assistance in February, March and April.

ii. The main reason seems to be purchase of fixtures and fittings.

iii. No income from debtors for first two months as two months' credit is allowed.

iv. Less cash purchases; more credit purchases.

Reasons: less resources. Probably one month credit allowed. More income from debtors.

22
Accounting Concepts

Accounting entity
(Or sometimes called **Business entity**) The fact that the business is a separate entity. It is separate from the owner. The owner must therefore have a separate bank account for his private use.

Accruals (matching)
The need to compare income and expenditure over the same period they were *incurred* not paid.

Consistency
Whatever accounting method is chosen, eg types of depreciation, the same method must continue to be used from year to year.

Continuity
(Or **going concern**). The assumption that the business will continue to trade.

Duality
Double entry. There is always another half to every entry, one debit and one credit.

Materiality
The way in which relatively small items are treated in the accounts, ie common sense prevails.

Money measurement
Transactions are always written up as amounts in money, but you need to be aware that it does not necessarily refer to the amount of cash in the business.

Prudence (conservatism)
The accountant always accounts for possible losses, but never overstates profits: cautious attitude.

Glossary

A/c. Abbreviation for account.

Account. A record of debits and credits which shows how much is owed.

Asset. Something owned by the business, eg premises, or an amount in favour of the business, eg rent paid in advance by the business. Includes anything owing to business.

Accounting concept. A rule of accountancy. There are many of these. The ones you need to know are listed in this book with explanations (see Contents).

Annum. Year.

Appropriation. Sharing out, distributing profits.

b/d. An abbreviation for **brought down**. It refers to the balance or amount left with which to continue the account.

B/fwd. An abbreviation for **brought forward**. Exactly the same as b/d. Either abbreviation may be used.

Balance. The amount on an account; the amount needed to close an account. To balance the books means to have everything correct and in agreement.

Book of original entry. The place where any transaction is first recorded. It is not usually part of the accounting system, just a record. The **cash book** is the exception as it is part of the system and also a book or original entry.

c/d. An abbreviation for **carried down**. It is written against the amount which will still be left on the account. Sometimes written as 'To c/d'.

C/fwd. Exactly the same as **c/d**. Either abbreviation may be used.

Capital. The amount of money the owner(s) put into the business. What the business owes the owner(s).

Capital employed. The total amount of capital plus net profit less drawings. It should be the same as net worth (see chapters on balance sheet and interpretation of final accounts).

Concept. In accounting terms this is one of the rules (see **accounting concept** above).

Credit. All transactions are said to be either debit or credit. To credit someone's account means that you owe them or they have paid you.

Debit. Loosely, this is something which is owned by or owed to the business. Note that debit and credit in accounting are different from the account you have with your bank.

Dishonoured cheque. A cheque which is returned when you have paid it into the bank. This will be for one of several reasons such as insufficient funds in drawer's account, no signature, not written out correctly and so on.

Drawer. The person on whose account a cheque will be drawn, ie the person who signed it, or the firm whose name appears under the signature.

Final accounts. Trading and profit and loss accounts, balance sheets.

Imprest. Float: amount of money kept in petty cash. Name given to system used for petty cash.

Liability. An expense or debt incurred by the business. Something that is owed by the business.

Net or nett. The final amount when all expenses/deductions have been made.

Payee. The person or firm to whom a cheque is made out— the recipient.

Posting. A term used in accounting to describe entering amounts on to the accounts.

Reconciliation. The act of making two things agree. The statement from the bank has to be reconciled with your own record. The purchase ledger accounts will have to be reconciled against the bills/demands/statements you get from suppliers.

Refer to drawer. This phrase of **r/d** will be stamped on a dishonoured cheque by the bank.

Revenue. Money. Sales revenue is money generated from sales. Revenue expenses are the regular yearly expenses.

Transaction. The act of selling or buying something.

Unpresented cheque. A cheque you have paid out, but which has not yet appeared on your bank statement.

Working capital. Current assets less current liabilities (see chapter on the balance sheet for explanation of these).

Addresses of Exam Boards

These are addresses of the examining boards for the GCSE exams.

The Associated Examining Board
  Stag Hill House
  Guildford
  Surrey GU2 5XJ.

Associated Lancashire Schools Exam Board
  12 Harter Street
  Manchester M16HL.

East Anglian Exam Board
  The Lindens
  Lexden Road
  Colchester
  Essex CO3 3RL.

East Midlands Regional Examinations Board
  Robins Wood House
  Robins Wood Road
  Aspley
  Nottingham NG3 3NR.

Joint Matriculation Board
  John Sherratt & Son Ltd
  78 Park Road
  Altrincham
  Cheshire WA14 5QQ.

London Regional Exam Board
  Lyon House

104 Wandsworth High Street
London SW18 4LF.

North Regional Examinations Board
  Wheatfield Road
  Westerhope
  Newcastle Upon Tyne NE5 5JZ.

North West Regional Exam Board
  Orbit House
  Albert Street
  Eccles
  Manchester M30 0WL.

Northern Ireland Schools Examinations Council
  Examinations Office
  Beechill House
  Beechill Road
  Belfast BT8 4RS.

Oxford and Cambridge Schools Examinations Board
  10 Trumpington Street
  Cambridge CB2 1QB.

Southern Universities Joint Board
  Cotham Road
  Bristol BS6 6DD.

University of Cambridge Local Exam Syndicate
  Syndicate Buildings
  Hills Road
  Cambridge CB1 2EU.

University of London School Exam Board
  52 Gordon Square
  London WC1E 6EE.

University of Oxford Delegacy of Local Exams
  Ewert Place
  Banbury Road
  Summertown
  Oxford OX2 7BZ.

Welsh Joint Education Committee
    245 Western Avenue
    Cardiff CF5 2YX.

West Midland Examinations Board
    Norfolk House
    Smallbrook
    Queensway
    Birmingham B5 4NJ.

Yorkshire and Humberside Regional Exam Board
    Scarsdale House
    136 Derbyshire Lane
    Sheffield S8 8SE.

Southern Regional Exam Board
    Avondale House
    33 Carlton Crescent
    Southampton
    Hants SO9 4YL.

South East Regional Examinations Board
    Beloe House
    2-10 Mount Ephraim Road
    Royal Tunbridge Wells
    Kent TN1 1EU.

South Western Examinations Board
    23-29 Marsh Street
    Bristol BS1 4BP.

Index

How to Employ & Manage Staff
Wendy Wyatt

This easy to use handbook will help all managers and supervisors
whose work involves them in recruiting and managing staff. Ideal for
quick reference, it provides a ready-made framework of modern
employment practice from recruitment onwards. It provides a clear
account of how to apply the health & safety at work regulations, how to
handle record-keeping, staff development, grievance and disciplinary
procedures, maternity and sick leave and similar matters for the benefit
of the organisation and its employees. The book includes a useful
summary of current employment legislation and is complete with a
range of model forms, letters, notices and similar documents. Wendy
Wyatt GradIPM is a Personnel Management and Employment
Consultant; her other books include *Recruiting Success* and *Jobhunt*,
and she has contributed regularly to the press on employment matters.
128pp illus. 0 7643 0554 0.

How to Know Your Rights at Work
Robert Spicer MA

Written in clear English, this easy-to-follow handbook sets out
everyone's rights at work whether in an office, shop, factory or
other setting. 'Justifiably described as a practical guide to employment
law. It is clearly written in language readily understood by the layman
. . . The text has been well laid out and sections are clearly
signposted . . . The extensive use of case study material is interesting
and helpful . . . The book is not only relevant to Careers Officers and
their clients, but also to other people working in the employment/
employment advisory field, eg. Citizens Advice Bureaux workers,
personnel officers, Trade Union Personnel, and indeed anyone wishing
to find out about their rights at work . . . The sort of book that can be
easily dipped into for specific information, but which is interesting
enough in its own right to be read from cover to cover.' *Careers Officer
Journal*. 'Sets out in simple English everything an employee can expect
in today's working environment.' *Kent Evening Post*. Robert Spicer
MA (Cantab) is a practising barrister, legal editor and author who
specialises in employment law. He was Editor of the Case Index on
Employment Law (Kluwer) and has taught law at Bristol University
and Bristol Polytechnic.
131pp. 1 85703 009 5.

How to Master Business English
Michael Bennie

Are you communicating effectively? Do your business documents achieve the results you want? Or are they too often ignored or misunderstood? Good communication is the key to success in any business. Whether you are trying to sell a product, answer a query or complaint, or persuade colleagues, the way you express yourself is often as important as what you say. With lots of examples, checklists and questionnaires to help you, this book will speed you on your way, whether as manager, executive, or business student. 'An excellent book—not in the least dull . . . Altogether most useful for anyone seeking to improve their communication skills.' *IPS Journal.* 'Gives guidance on writing styles for every situation . . . steers the reader through the principles and techniques of effective letter-writing and document-planning.' *First Voice.* 'Useful chapters on grammar, punctuation and spelling. Frequent questionnaires and checklists enable the reader to check progress.' *Focus (Society of Business Teachers).* Michael Bennie is a Director of Studies of the Department of Business Writing of Writers College, and author of *How to Do Your Own Advertising* in this series.
208pp illus. 0 7463 0582 6

How to Master Public Speaking
Anne Nicholls

Speaking well in public is one of the most useful skills any of us can acquire. People who can often become leaders in their business, profession or community, and the envy of their friends and colleagues. Whether you are a nervous novice or a practised pro, this step-by-step handbook tells you everything you need to know to master this highly prized communication skill. Contents: Preface, being a skilled communicator, preparation, researching your audience, preparing a speech, finding a voice, body language and non-verbal communication, dealing with nerves, audiovisual aids, the physical environment, putting it all together on the day, audience feedback, dealing with the media, glossary, further reading, useful contacts, index. Anne Hulbert Nicholls BA(Hons) PGCE was a Lecturer in Communications and Journalism in a College of Education for 14 years and ran courses in Presentation Skills and Effective Speaking for local business people. She now runs seminars and conferences for a publishing company and writes articles for a number of national magazines and newspapers. Her articles

appear regularly in *Living* magazine. She has also worked in Public
Relations and for BBC Radio.
160pp illus. 0 7463 0521 4.

How to Write a Report
John Bowden

Communicating effectively on paper is an essential skill for today's
business or professional person, for example in managing an
organisation, dealing with staffing, sales and marketing, production,
computer operations, financial planning and reporting, feasibility
studies and business innovation. Written by an experienced manager
and staff trainer, this well-presented handbook provides a very clear
step-by-step framework for every individual, whether dealing with
professional colleagues, customers, clients, suppliers or junior or senior
staff. John Bowden BSc(Econ) MSc studied at the London School of
Economics. He has long experience both as a professional manager in
industry, and as a Senior Lecturer running courses in accountancy,
auditing, and effective communication, up to senior management level.
160pp illus. 1 85703 035 4. Reprinted.

How to Publish a Newsletter
Graham Jones

Are you planning a community newsletter, business bulletin, house
magazine, school newspaper or similar publication? With so many
design and print facilities around today there has probably never been a
better time to start. This practical book takes you in easy steps through
the whole process, starting with how to get the initial concept right.
Then, using examples and helpful checklists throughout, it shows how
to design a workable format, how to finance the costs of publication by
subscriptions, advertising and other means, how to edit text and
illustrations and handle contributors, how to write using a house style,
how to prepare layouts and artwork and deal with the printer, and how
to organise effective distribution. Graham Jones is Managing Director
of ASPECT, a company which produces house magazines and other
publications for client organisations.
176pp illus. 1 85703 032 5.

How to Pass That Interview
Judith Johnstone

Everyone knows how to shine at interview—or do they? When every candidate becomes the perfect clone of the one before, you need that extra 'something' to raise your chances above the rest. Using a systematic and practical approach, this new How To book takes you step-by-step through the essential pre-interview groundwork, the interview encounter itself, and what you can learn from the experience afterwards. The book contains sample pre- and post-interview correspondence, and is complete with a guide to further reading, glossary of terms, and index. Judith Johnstone has written extensively on employment-related subjects. A Graduate of the Institute of Personnel Management, she has been an instructor in Business Studies and adult literacy tutor, and has long experience of helping people at work.
128pp illus. 1 85703 004 4. Reprinted.

How to Keep Business Accounts
Peter Taylor
Second Edition

A new revised edition of an easy-to-understand handbook for all business owners and managers. 'Will help you sort out the best way to carry out double entry book-keeping, as well as providing a clear step-by-step guide to accounting procedures.' *Mind Your Own Business*. 'Progresses through the steps to be taken to maintain an effective double entry book-keeping system with the minimum of bother.' *The Accounting Technician*. 'Compulsory reading.' *Manager, National Westminster Bank (Midlands)*. Peter Taylor is a Fellow of the Institute of Chartered Accountants, and of the Chartered Association of Certified Accountants. He has many years' practical experience of advising small businesses.
176pp illus. 0 7463 0618 0.

How to Master Book-Keeping
An Introduction for Students
Peter Marshall

Book-keeping can seem a confusing subject for people coming to it for the first time. This very clear book will be welcomed by everyone

wanting a really user-friendly guide to recording business transactions step-by-step. Illustrated at every stage with specimen entries, the book will also be an ideal companion for students taking LCCI, RSA, BTEC, accountancy technician and similar courses at schools, colleges or training centres. Typical business transactions are used to illustrate all the essential theory, practice and skills required to be effective in a real business setting. Contents: Preface, introduction, theory of double entry, day books, cash book, bank reconciliation, petty cash book, journal, postage book, the ledger, discounts, control accounts, trial balance, accruals and prepayments, revenue accounts, the balance sheet, manufacturing accounts, depreciation, bad and doubtful debts, partnership and accounts, amalgamation of sole proprietorships into a partnership, limited companies, 'going limited', reflection, club accounts, asset disposals, correction of errors, VAT accounts, incomplete records, interpretation of accounts, wages, stock records. Peter Marshall BSc(Econ) BA(Hons) FRSA FSBT MBIM has been Tutor in Education at the University of Lancaster and Director of Studies at the Careers College, Cardiff. He has contributed regularly to *FOCUS on Business Education*.
176pp illus. 1 85703 022 2.

How to Raise Business Finance
Peter Ibbetson

Every business needs to raise money from time to time. It may be for start-up capital, to cover a difficult cash flow, to invest in research and development, to finance new equipment, premises, or exports, or to restructure the business as a whole. Written by a professional banker, this highly readable book explains what finance costs, what base rates and APR mean, how fixed interest loans work. It discusses where cash can be found in a business, for example from existing debtors/creditors, as well as outside lenders. It considers the importance of the balance sheet, track record, gearing, overheads, project viability, and the importance of cash flow forecasting (explaining why this may differ markedly from profit forecasts). Equity financing and management buyouts are explained too, and the role of financial institutions and government sources summarised. Whole chapters are devoted to special forms of finance such as leasing, factoring, contract hire, and finance for exporters, backed up with pages of key references, contacts and addresses, and a helpful glossary of financial and banking terms. 'Gives the right amount of information.' *Association of British Chambers of Commerce*. 'A lucid account of the steps by which a small businessman can substantially strengthen his case.' *The Financial Times*. Peter

Ibbetson is an Associate of the Chartered Institute of Bankers, and an author and broadcaster on banking matters.
160pp illus. 07463 0338 6.

How to Invest in Stocks and Shares
Dr John White

This book has been specially prepared to help and guide those with a substantial sum to invest (often more than £50,000) and who are considering investing all or part of this sum in quoted securities. Often such investors have such a sum as a result of a recent inheritance, for example when the house of a deceased parent has been sold. This new book recognises that such investors are not normally interested in suspect get-rich-quick schemes, but rather in a practical and level-headed approach in which longterm objectives are important. This book therefore provides a complete step-by-step framework to share selection and dealing, and portfolio management, against a background of longer term trends. Dr John White, an Oxford graduate, is himself an experienced investor and adviser to an investment company. He has a professional background in computers and has produced a range of software for chart analysis.
192pp illus. 1 85703 036 2.

How to Start a Business from Home
Graham Jones
Second Edition

Most people have dreamed of starting their own business from home at some time or other; but how do you begin? What special skills do you need? This great value-for-money paperback has the answers, showing how you can profit from your own talents and experience, and start turning spare time into cash from the comfort of your own home. *How to Start a Business From Home* contains a wealth of ideas, projects, tips, facts, checklists and quick-reference information for everyone—whether in between jobs, taking early retirement, or students and others with time to invest. Packed with information on everything from choosing a good business idea and starting up to advertising, book-keeping and dealing with professionals, this book is essential reading for every budding entrepreneur. 'Full of ideas and advice.' *The Daily Mirror.*

Graham Jones BSc(Hons) is an editor, journalist and lecturer specialising in practical business subjects. His other books include *Fit to Manage* and *The Business of Freelancing*.
176pp. 1 85703 012 5.

How to Do Your Own Advertising
Michael Bennie

'Entrepreneurs and small businesses are flooding the market with new products and services; the only way to beat the competition is successful selling—and that means advertising.' But what can you afford? This book is for anyone who needs—or wants—to advertise effectively, but does not want to pay agency rates. It will also be useful to those who simply want to know what is involved in advertising, whether as students, business people or interested laymen. What are the secrets of putting together effective ads? Even the basic design can be done by someone with a little imagination and creativity. This book shows you step-by- step how to assemble a simple, straightforward, yet highly successful ad or brochure with the minimum of outside help. Every step is clearly explained with the beginner in mind. There are numerous illustrations, lots of examples of actual ads, a variety of case studies to show the principles in practice and the aim throughout is to make advertising easy and enjoyable. Complete with questionnaires and checklists to help you check your progress. Michael Bennie has had many years' professional experience as a Sales Manager with a number of international companies, covering all aspects of sales and copywriting. He is now a freelance copywriter and advertising consultant, and Director of Studies at the Copywriting School.
176pp illus. 0 7463 0579 6.